DO GOOD, BE GREAT

DO GOOD, BE GREAT

Discovering the Keys to Unlocking the Greatness in You

Scott George

ISBN: 1535545720
ISBN 13: 9781535545723
Library of Congress Control Number: 2016912652
CreateSpace Independent Publishing Platform
North Charleston, South Carolina

Table of Contents

Foreword

By Orlando Magic's Pat Williams

For the past 45 years I have had the honor of observing, meeting, interviewing and writing about great leaders in our world; great men and women in our generation who have impacted and influenced millions of people and made our lives better. Leaders like John Wooden, Billy Graham, Mother Teresa, Vince Lombardi and Abraham Lincoln. With over 100 books that I have written over the years I have highlighted their character, integrity and keys for their success. My books have focused on the principles, keys and secrets that have shaped their lives and made them who they are. One life lesson that has surfaced time and time again and that I have noticed is consistent in all effective leaders is the power of goodness that they possess. Goodness precedes greatness, and when people live a life of goodness it opens the way for greatness follow. When you find a person who can do good they will be great.

Scott George, over the past 30 years, has proven this principle and lives a life of goodness. In his new exciting book, *"Do good . . . Be Great,"* Scott highlights incredible leaders of our past and in our world today who have illustrated the principle of do good be great. Leaders like Bono, Bill Gates, Oprah, Mother Teresa and Martin Luther King, who have a lasting legacy of moving from good to great by living lives of vision, integrity and compassion. This wonderful book will not only inspire you and motivate you to live a life of goodness, but it will challenge you to apply the keys that can change you, impact others and make you great. If you're content with average, status quo and vanilla living, his book isn't for you; but if you desire to learn from the world's great leaders and allow their stories of kindness, compassion and inspiration to give you the fuel you need to move forward and make our world better, this book will stir up the goodness in you so that greatness can come alive in you and change our world.

Pat Williams
Orlando Magic Senior Vice President

Great Quotes from a Great Leader
Pope Francis

- *"Among our tasks as witnesses to the love of Christ is that of giving a voice to the cry of the poor, so that they are not abandoned to the laws of an economy that seems at times to treat people as mere consumers."*
- *"[Embrace] poverty learned with the humble, the poor, the sick and all those who are on the existential peripheries of life. Theoretical poverty is of no use to us. Poverty is learned by touching the flesh of the poor Christ, in the humble, the poor, the sick, in children."*
- *"Men and women are sacrificed to the idols of profit and consumption: It is the 'culture of waste.' If you break a computer it is a tragedy; but poverty, the needs, the dramas of so many people end up becoming the norm."*
- *"Grace is not part of consciousness; it is the amount of light in our souls, not knowledge or reason."*
- *"To encounter the living God it is necessary to tenderly kiss Jesus' wounds in our hungry, poor, sick, and incarcerated brothers and sisters."*
- *"It means protecting people, showing loving concern for each and every person, especially children, the elderly, those in need—who are often the last we think about."*
- *"Even the weakest and most vulnerable, the sick, the old, the unborn and the poor, are masterpieces of God's creation, made in his own image, destined to live forever, and deserving of the utmost reverence and respect."*
- *"These two criteria are like the pillars of true love: deeds and the gift of self."*

1

In All Ways Big and Small – Do Good, Be Great

KEY 1: BEYOND ORDINARY PEOPLE SWEAT THE SMALL STUFF

Pope Francis—Do Good, Be Great Leading the Catholic Church

Shortly after his historic election in 2013 as the 266th pontiff of the Roman Catholic Church, Pope Francis sat for a six-hour interview with the prestigious Jesuit magazine, *Civiltà Cattolica*. It was his first major media appearance as pope. The Rome-based publication was effectively introducing the new Holy Father to the world. One thing the magazine wanted to know was why Francis, upon looking at the traditional papal residence on the third floor of the Apostolic Palace, had decided he would not live there.

"The papal apartment is old, tastefully decorated, and large, but not luxurious," he began his answer. "But the entrance is really tight . . . like an inverted funnel." Then, with a candor he's come to be known for, he revealed his reason for rejecting the historic flat. "People can come only in dribs and drabs, and I cannot live without people. I need to live my life with others." By revealing his need to live "life with others," Francis gave the world a glimpse into why he is today known as a pope of the people who is reforming the Catholic Church according to his strong social conscience. Francis's personal history as a Roman Catholic cleric is one of championing the Church's outreaches even more than her doctrines. For the majority of his life, the seventy-eight-year-old Argentinean has been a pioneer for the poor, a voice for the voiceless, and a tireless advocate for humanitarian assistance and economic justice for the needy and oppressed.

Even his choice of "Francis" as his papal name was meant to honor the patron saint of the poor, St. Francis of Assisi. He selected it to emphasize the responsibility of the Church to protect and defend the poor. "[St. Francis] loved, helped, and served the needy, the sick, and the poor," he says. "This is what I want; a poor Church for the poor." His stated mission is to rebuild the Church as "a place of mercy and hope, where everyone is welcomed, loved, and forgiven."

Pope Francis was born Jorge Mario Bergoglio on December 17, 1936, in Buenos Aires, Argentina, the son of Italian immigrants. His father, Mario, was an accountant with the railroads, and his mother, Regina, stayed home to raise the couple's large family. As a young man, Jorge had a fondness for *milonga*, the traditional music and dancing of Argentina and Uruguay.

He grew to have a strong background in education, becoming fluent in Spanish, German, and Italian, and earning a master's degree in chemistry. He had started a career as a chemical technician when he chose the clergy over career and entered Villa Devoto seminary in Buenos Aires and the Company of Jesus in 1958. Ordained a priest in 1969, he served in succession as a professor of theology, rector, and parish priest. In 1992, he was appointed Bishop of Buenos Aires by Pope John Paul II. In 1998, he succeeded Cardinal Antonio Quarracino to become Archbishop of Buenos Aires and lead a diocese of more than 3 million people.

Archbishop Bergoglio was known as a simple pastor, well-loved by his diocese. He lived frugally, used public transportation, and kept a modest residence where he cooked his own meals. His answer to those who questioned why, as an archbishop, he opted for a humble lifestyle was: "My people are poor, and I am one of them." He advised his priests always to show mercy and keep their doors open to everyone. "Being self-centered," he warned, "is the worst thing that could happen to the Church."

During his fifteen years as Archbishop of Buenos Aires, he strengthened the presence of the Church in the slums and underdeveloped neighborhoods of the city, doubling the number of priests working the areas. Passionate to be among his people, Francis made it his custom on Holy Thursday, before Easter, to be in a jail, a hospital, a home for the elderly, or with the poor to observe the Church's ritual washing of feet.

In 2001, John Paul II selected him as a cardinal. On March 13, 2013, he was elected pope, becoming the first pontiff to replace a living pope in more than 600 years, as well as the first Jesuit pope, and the first pope from the Americas.

As a pope of significant "firsts" in Roman Catholic history, Francis is showing the world that he is serious about his first mission: reforming the Church. One key way he is going about this is by naming cardinals from the so-called peripheries of the modern world. He is expected to name 125 cardinals and has started by picking ones from places such as Cape Verde, Ethiopia, Myanmar, Panama, Tonga, and Uruguay.

His selections are noteworthy because they have empowered the voices and experiences of those who have been largely excluded from governance and decision-making authority. His reforms are in keeping with who he is as a spiritual figurehead. He prefers to be known for feeding and clothing the oppressed of the world rather than for his high office.

Today the newest pope lives at Domus Sanctae Marthae, a residence building for clerics and official Vatican guests, close to Saint Peter's Basilica. He occupies a modest, three-room suite and takes his meals in a common dining room. The traditional papal quarters in the Apostolic Palace are reserved instead only for official receptions and meetings with heads of state. Pope Francis demonstrates that to do Good and be Great is best achieved when leaders are willing not just to lead but also to serve.

"The people of God want pastors, not clergy acting like bureaucrats or government officials," Francis told *Civiltà Cattolica* during their interview. "I see the Church as a field hospital after battle. It is useless to ask a seriously injured person if he has high cholesterol. You have to heal his wounds. Then we can talk about everything else. You have to start from the ground up."

Pope Francis has made a dramatic impact, not only in the Catholic Church, but the entire world, both Christian and secular. From the moment he was anointed to become the leader of the largest organization in the world, he began to make several changes that have had incredible impact, not only on the structure of the Catholic Church, but the perception of those outside the church, as well. Small, yet profound changes, from where he resides to how he travels, from his security personnel to his spending—each small detail after another has yielded incredible change. The ripple effect of little changes can impact the world, and Pope Francis has modeled this "great" to perfection.

Pope Francis is obviously a man who is living to do Good, and be Great. Hundreds of millions of people around the world are impacted by his vision, leadership, and compassion. In the Introduction, you met a greater person who, although not quite as popular as Pope Francis, was living a life beyond ordinary to do Good and be Great. Her name is Tabitha. Let's drill down a bit more together and see how she lived a life to do Good, be Great by looking to the New Testament account found in Acts 9:36-42 (NIV)

Tabitha—Do Good, Be Great

In Joppa there was a disciple named Tabitha (in Greek her name is Dorcas); she was always doing good and helping the poor. About that time she became sick and died, and her body was washed and placed in an upstairs room. Lydda was near Joppa; so when the disciples heard that Peter was in Lydda, they sent two men to him and urged him, "Please come at once!" Peter went with them, and when he arrived he was taken upstairs to the room. All the widows stood around him, crying and showing him the robes and other clothing that Dorcas had made while she was still with them. Peter sent them all out of the room; then he got down on his knees and prayed. Turning toward the dead woman, he said, "Tabitha, get up." She opened her eyes, and seeing Peter she sat up. He took her by the hand and helped her to her feet. Then he called for the believers, especially the widows, and presented her to them alive. This became known all over Joppa, and many people believed in the Lord. (Acts 9:36-42, NIV)

All the widows stood around him, crying and showing him the robes and other clothing that Dorcas had made while she was still with them. (Acts 9:39, NIV)

In that obscure little town outside the ancient city of Tel Aviv, a room filled with women wept because of their loss. Despite every prayer, every cry, and every tear, the women's hurt, hopelessness, and desperation would not dissipate. The widows had experienced pain before, but never like that. Little did they know, that day something would happen that would change their lives. It was the day death would again be defeated, goodness would win, and their hope would be restored.

She became sick and died, and her body was washed and placed in an upstairs room. (Acts 9:37, NIV)

History tells us that it was a normal day for this woman named Tabitha. Culturally, she would have started out very early in the morning with chores, meals, and all the tasks that had to be done, before the hustle and bustle of the day began. Chances are this woman of lore did not have a family with children. So there were no lunches to pack, homework to check, or meals to prepare before school started.

Most likely, she did not have a husband to chat with before the start of a busy day or a last minute shirt to iron before the man of the house headed out for the all-important business meeting. She was probably a widow, a single woman in a culture known for marriage, family, children, and grandchildren. None of that was in her future, and she knew it. Down deep she knew she would be ridiculed, rejected, and scorned by some. Yet despite the shame she felt each day, she was determined to look beyond the hurt and live a life of deep purpose and meaning. But this was no normal day. This was the day of destiny for her, a day that would change the course of history for her and generations to come.

Peter sent them all out of the room; then he got down on his knees and prayed. Turning toward the dead woman, he said, "Tabitha, get up." (Acts 9:40, NIV)

Just looking around the room, anyone could see Tabitha was consumed with a purpose and deep mission. Everywhere there was evidence of the selfless work she did for others. It was quite a bit more than just a business she was running; it was much more than that.

As visitors walked into the room they could sense her life was filled with destiny and determination; her small, secluded house in the rural countryside was normally filled with activity of another kind. It was the place where Tabitha made clothes for those who were cold and abandoned. It was the place where people in need—the hungry, lonely, and afraid— would come for help.

She was known all over the region as the one to go to for help when your back was against the wall. She would be there for you. You could count on her for help. Now she was the one who needed help. It was her back that was "against the wall"—for she lay motionless and unresponsive on her bed.

She opened her eyes, and seeing Peter she sat up. (Acts 9:40, NIV)

The prayers had been answered. The tears had not been in vain. The cries had been heard. It was the greatest day in Joppa's history. People would talk about this for years. Grandparents would tell this story for generations. The underdog won. Good people finished first. Goodness prevailed. A prayer changed a life. A prayer changed the city. A prayer changed the country. Tabitha became a living legend in a day. The one they said was "always doing good and helping the poor" (Acts 9:36, NIV), was a hero.

If we choose to live in the legacy of Pope Francis or Tabitha, we will soon discover that they share life principles in common, and qualities we too must possess if we are going to do Good, Great. I call these life principles "keys for living beyond ordinary." They are the keys we need to live by in order to do Good, Great. Let's look at the first key: How to Sweat the Small Stuff.

5 Things I Wish Someone Had Told Me about Sweating the Small Stuff

1. Little Things Matter

The first key I wish someone would have told me about sweating the small stuff is that little things matter. Many times we get so focused on the big picture that we lose sight of the small stuff. For years, it is likely you heard the saying, "Don't sweat the small stuff." This old saying may sound cute, but its influence has a dynamic impact on your life and destiny. A story told by Brian Tracy illustrates best the power of little things in our lives.

Brian described two salesmen going head-to-head in a role-played sales contest. The winner needed to earn 100 points. Both men were well-groomed (worth 5 points) and appropriately dressed (worth 8 points). They both kept appointments and followed up as requested (worth 4 points). Each was knowledgeable about the products (worth 6 points) and gave remarkable presentations (worth 10 points). With the evaluations nearly complete, the salesmen were tied at 99 points each. One more factor was taken into account—their pens. One used a Cross pen throughout his presentation (worth 2 points); the other used a Bic pen, which had no point value. The salesman with the Cross pen won the contest.

One little thing made the difference between winning and losing a sale. One little thing, seemingly insignificant, separated one salesman from the other. One little thing mattered.[1]

I love what Coach Wooden, the great basketball coach and successful leader, says about sweating the small stuff: "It's the little details that are vital. Little things make big things happen" (Coach John Wooden).

Dwight L. Moody, the world-famous Christian leader, echoes the words of Coach Wooden by saying, "There are many of us that are willing to do great things for the Lord, but few of us are willing to do little things."

2. Little Things Have Big Impact

Have you ever had a toothache? If so, you know that the pain starts very simply at first, but if left alone, increases in intensity. Little things unnoticed can cause tremendous discomfort, pain, and even agony.

Some of this book I wrote while speaking and teaching at a conference in Zambia, an African country. I was there to teach leaders and pastors about leadership and the power of leading with integrity and character. On that trip, while traveling to Mozambique for a leadership conference there, the car I was driving broke down. It turned out a very small part of the air-conditioning system was at fault. This breakdown had a big impact on our schedule and affected thousands of people attending the leadership conference. Although the part was only the size of a quarter, it made a big difference!

Don't underestimate the influence of small things. They matter in your life, business, charity, marriage, and future. I like what Kareem Abdul-Jabbar once said: "I try to do the right thing at the right time. They may just be little things, but usually they make the difference between winning and losing." Mother Teresa once wisely said of small things: "We can do no great things; only small things with great love."

3. Become a CDO—Chief Details Officer

The world has been affected in a major way by the vision of Walt Disney. Here in Orlando, my hometown, his influence is hard to imagine. Every time I set foot on the property of Walt Disney World and enter the gates, I marvel, thinking *This man had an incredible vision and attention to detail.*

Pat Williams, senior vice president of the Orlando Magic, and a gifted leader from the Orlando area, tells how Walt Disney was the "chief detail officer" on a minute-by-minute basis. Walt Disney's practiced eye never missed a detail.

One time, his animation staff produced some footage of a Mickey Mouse cartoon for Walt's approval. Just to test Walt, they cut the tail off Mickey in a single frame of the cartoon. Cartoons are projected at a rate of twenty-four frames per second, so that single image of a tailless Mickey flashed by Walt's eyes in 1/24 of a second. Walt watched the entire cartoon without saying a word and the animators thought he had missed the tailless frame. But as soon as the cartoon was over, Walt said, "It'll work—but put the tail back on Mickey before you release it."[2]

"Big things are accomplished only through the perfection of minor details." (Coach John Wooden)

4. One is Not the Loneliest Number

I'm sure you've heard of the famous song "One" by Three Dog Night ("One is the loneliest number . . ."). I love that song and the lyrics, but after looking at leaders and the world, I've come to discover that *one* is not a lonely number at all. In fact, I wish someone would have told me that one number, one person, one voice, one leader, or one call can make a dynamic difference.

Read the following results from political elections from the past and you will see that *one* is not a lonely number at all:

In 1645, one vote gave Oliver Cromwell control of England.

In 1649, one vote caused Charles I of England to be executed.

In 1776, one vote determined that English, not German, would be the American language.

In 1845, one vote brought Texas into the Union.

In 1868, one vote saved President Andrew Johnson from impeachment.

In 1875, one vote changed France from a monarchy to a republic.

In 1923, one vote gave Hitler control of the Nazi party.

In 1941, twelve weeks before Pearl Harbor, one vote saved the Selective Service.

In 1960, Richard Nixon lost the presidential election, and John F. Kennedy won it by less than one vote per precinct in the United States.[3]

I've seen this a few times before in books and leadership magazines. Some may question the facts of these results, but nevertheless, they remind me of the importance of sweating the small stuff.

5. *Small Foxes Spoil the Vine*

If you're like me, you heard a few very famous sayings when you were younger that stuck with you over the years. Here's one I've heard before, as I'm sure you have: "One bad apple spoils the whole bunch." My grandfather George used to tell me this one all the time as he tried to impart wisdom to his rowdy grandson: "Scotty, small foxes spoil the vine." To be honest with you, I never really understood what he was talking about until I grew up and one day read in the Bible this quote from Solomon, *"Take us the foxes, the little foxes, that spoil the vines: for our vines have tender grapes"* (Song of Solomon 2:15, KJV, underline added).

Someone once said, "He who never quotes is never quoted." My grandfather George was a wise man who became wiser by learning to use quotes from other wise men. You'll see in this book that I have used the same methodology, offering quotes and wisdom from people wiser than me. My grandfather was smart enough to use the wisdom of Solomon to tell his oldest grandson that the small foxes (things) can spoil the vine. Solomon was crying out with his incredible wisdom to you and me by saying that we overlook the little things in life, but it's the small things that sneak in unnoticed, and little by little, ruin the whole crop.

If you want to live a beyond ordinary life, then one of the first keys I would encourage you to pursue is the mastery of small details. Become like Walt Disney, D. L. Moody, and Coach Wooden by developing the eye for small things. Make it a point today to become a CDO—Chief Detail Officer—who concentrates on and sweats the small stuff! You will quickly discover that in order to live the beyond ordinary life, you must not overlook the small things.

Questions for you on ....
Chapter 1: In All Ways Big and Small - Do Good, Be Great

1. When you read about Pope Francis, what are some of the do good be great qualities you see?

2. Pick out one of the quotes from Pope Francis and discuss why this particular quote inspires you.

3. In what ways did Tabitha's do good heart make her great?

4. When it comes to sweating the small stuff, what are some little areas in you that you are overlooking?

5. If small foxes spoil the vine, what little thing could you be doing right now that would move you from good to great?

6. You're now the CDO – Chief Detail Officer – of your corporation. What details will you begin to deal with so that you can be great at doing good?

Notes

Great Quotes from a Great Leader
Mother Teresa

- *"We think sometimes that poverty is only being hungry, naked, and homeless. The poverty of being unwanted, unloved, and uncared for is the greatest poverty. We must start in our own homes to remedy this kind of poverty."*
- *"Being unwanted, unloved, uncared for, forgotten by everybody: I think that is a much greater hunger, a much greater poverty than the person who has nothing to eat."*
- *"The person who gives with a smile is the best giver because God loves a cheerful giver."*
- *"Our life of poverty is as necessary as the work itself. Only in heaven will we see how much we owe to the poor for helping us to love God better because of them. "*
- *"Never worry about numbers. Help one person at a time and always start with the person nearest you."*
- *"What can you do to promote world peace? Go home and love your family. "*
- *"It's not how much we give but how much love we put into giving. "*
- *"Live simply so others may simply live."*
- *"If you can't feed a hundred people, then feed just one."*
- *"If you judge people, you have no time to love them."*
- *"Intense love does not measure; it just gives."*

2

Discover Your Destiny To Do Good, Be Great

KEY 2: BEYOND ORDINARY PEOPLE DAILY DISCOVER THEIR DESTINY

Mother Teresa—Do Good, Be Great for Those Hurting and Hopeless

The story is told that when Agnes Bojaxhiu decided at age eighteen to become a nun and dedicate her life to God in missionary service in India, her older brother was incensed with her. He was a prominent officer in the Army whose rank afforded him social status, respect, and a name people regarded. His sister's decision, he felt, would lead her only to an obscure life wasted on petty pursuits.

"Why don't you *make something* of your life!" Lieutenant Lazar Bojaxhiu is said to have shouted at Agnes. Undeterred by his chiding, Agnes moved forward and followed her dream. Fifty-one years later, in 1979, Lazar reportedly was in attendance for the ceremony in Oslo, Norway, when Agnes was awarded the Nobel Peace Prize for her astounding missionary service among India's poor. It is unlikely that any of us today would remotely recognize his name if we heard it. But Agnes's name, we all know. The name of Mother Teresa is known the world over. She was born Agnes Gomxha Bojaxhiu on August 26, 1910, in Skopje, a predominantly Muslim city in the Balkans. Agnes was the third and final child of Nikola and Dranafile Bojaxhiu, devout Albanian Catholics.

She was only twelve when she first felt an inescapable desire to serve God above anything else in life. She had read much about the work of Catholic missionaries in India and was determined to go there herself and do the same. She pondered her decision for six more years, during which time her father died and life for the family became harder.

Finally, in September 1928, Agnes could wait no longer and said good-bye to her family. She joined the Sisters of Loreto, an order of nuns based in Ireland with missions in India.

Agnes arrived in India in 1929, took her religious vows as a nun in 1931, and chose the name Teresa after Therese de Lisieux, the patron saint of missionaries. She began her service by teaching history and geography at the Loreto Convent School in Calcutta, but the poverty she witnessed everywhere outside the convent walls disturbed her greatly.

In 1937, "Sister Teresa" took her final vows and became "Mother Teresa." In 1946, while traveling 400 miles by train from Calcutta to Darjeeling, she received what she has since described as a "call within a call"—a summons she believes indisputably came from God Himself.

She recounts: "I was quietly praying when I clearly felt a call. The message was very clear: I had to leave the convent and consecrate myself to helping the poor by living among them. It was a command."

For two years, Mother Teresa petitioned the Church for permission to go to "the poorest of the poor." Sending a single woman alone into the slums of Calcutta seemed to her superiors to be irresponsible and dangerous on their part—and futile on hers. Her request, however, was sent to Rome and in August 1948, at age thirty-eight, Mother Teresa left the convent with the blessing of the Vatican to begin her missionary work with the poor. Before leaving, she purchased three cheap, white, cotton saris, each lined on the edge with three blue stripes. The simple wrap is today the iconic image she is known for—and it would become the uniform for Missionaries of Charity, the order of nuns she later founded to serve the poor.

She had no income her first year in the slums and resorted to begging for food and supplies. Doubt, loneliness, and the temptation to quit and return to convent life ceaselessly challenged her commitment. But the need, particularly among the dying, could not be ignored. For many Hindus, death was believed to be a contaminant of the place where it occurred. Often, those in the terminal stages of their illnesses were simply shoved out the door to die on a street, in a gutter, or wherever they might end up.

It was to these nearly dead castaways that Mother Teresa personally gave herself. She would lift them from the gutters and hail taxis or rickshaws to take them to hospitals. If the coachmen refused due to the putrid condition of the dying, she herself would put the person into a wheelbarrow and go in search of a hospital that would accept hopeless cases.

In 1950, she received permission from the Vatican to start the Missionaries of Charity, whose stated purpose was to seek out "the poorest, the abandoned, the sick, the infirm, the leprosy patients, the dying, the desperate, the lost, the outcasts; taking care of them . . . living Christ's love for them."

In 1952, she opened a home for the dying—Nirmal Hriday, Bengali for "Pure Heart." She and her nuns would walk the streets daily to bring them to the home, where they would be bathed, fed, and allowed to die with dignity. Mother Teresa started her order with twelve members. At the time of her death on September 5, 1997, the sisters of the Missionaries of Charity numbered 3,914 and were established in 594 communities in 123 countries. They care for refugees, the blind, disabled, aged, poor and homeless, as well as victims of floods, epidemics, and famine. More than 100,000 volunteers aid them. Her work continues today, and the order has grown to more than 4,000 members in 697 foundations in 131 countries.

As one whose devotion to do good, be Great was unmatched, Mother Teresa received 124 national and international awards of recognition, including the Templeton Prize in 1973, the Order of Merit (from Queen Elizabeth) in 1983, and the US Congressional Gold Medal in 1997.

When she accepted the Nobel award on that day in Oslo in 1979, she requested her $192,000 in prize money be given to the poor in India, telling the committee: "(Jesus) died for you and for me and for that leper and for that man dying of hunger and that naked person lying in the street. We are to share that passion." Mother Teresa was not just a saint who was a hero to hundreds of thousands of people; she was a humble servant who had an amazing ability to discover her God-given talent and then use it both to benefit the poor in Calcutta and to inspire missions and the global community.

There is another woman who, like Mother Teresa, lived a beyond ordinary life; but unlike Mother Teresa, she was relatively unknown and unnoticed. Hers wasn't a household name, but she lived an incredible life. We don't know very much about her, but what we do know shows us her life was filled with significance, purpose, and destiny.

We read about her in the Introduction. Her name was Tabitha. Although Mother Teresa and Tabitha lived hundreds of years apart and grew up in different parts of the world, they had much in common—namely, they both discovered the key of fulfilling their destiny and purpose.

What is Do Good, Be Great?

Tabitha's incredible story is documented in the New Testament. Her story has largely gone unnoticed and overlooked by many, and even deemed insignificant in the eyes of some. For centuries, readers have quickly glanced over this brief story and moved on to the bigger, more glamorous sections in the Bible that are popular and perhaps more thrilling to read.

History records her life with this seventeen-word description: *"In Joppa there was a disciple named Tabitha (in Greek her name is Dorcas); she was always doing good and helping the poor"* (Acts 9:36, NIV). Most people have never heard of her, let alone know about the amazing story of how this inconspicuous widow lived her life, always doing good and helping the poor, and how she was miraculously brought back from death to life in an instant.

We can all relate to a feeling of being overlooked, unnoticed, and lost in the big scheme of things. This story can inspire us to move beyond our current status and believe for a life of purpose, significance, and meaning.

The hero and main character of this "one of a kind story" is Tabitha. "Tabitha" is just a normal name, not fancy or spectacular. If I were to think of the name of a leading lady for a movie, it wouldn't be "Tabitha." However, it turns out her name was perfect for the script of this story. Tabitha's name means, *"gazelle."* She was from the small town of Joppa. Joppa historically means *"beautiful"* . . . Tabitha from Joppa . . . *"beautiful gazelle."* I think you're starting to get the picture.

When I think of beautiful gazelle, I think of grace, speed, and agility. My mind immediately goes to the *National Geographic* programs that I often watch on TV. Usually the scene is from Africa, where the scenery is majestic and the stunning views take your breath away. The gazelle is poetry in motion as it moves effortlessly through the fields, uninhibited and free, until the lion is introduced into the story. Suddenly the peaceful scene goes south quickly, and you watch as the beautiful gazelle runs for its life. There's fear and panic in its eyes, and anxiety in your heart as you watch and secretly cheer for the gazelle to escape.

Nature shadows life. We are at our best when, like Tabitha, we are the beautiful gazelle running through life, filled with purpose, passion, and significance—poetry in motion. However, when a crisis finds its way into our lives, like the fear-panicked gazelle, we suddenly run for our lives with an enemy not far behind.

Jewish history records how this beautiful gazelle named Tabitha was always doing good and helping the poor. Once tagged, for her entire life this label followed her. It followed her anytime others spoke of her or discussed her.

I can hear the street vendors in Joppa speaking of her as I write these pages, "Oh yes, Tabitha . . . the one who is always doing good and helping the poor." I can see her schoolteacher sitting down with her parents at the annual parent-teacher conference and describing Tabitha as "the one who was always doing good and helping her classmates." If her senior classmates had voted like we do today, for "best looking" or "most popular," she might have been left out of the voting. They do not typically heap accolades on the "most compassionate" or "most likely to help the underdog."

What an amazing label to have follow you wherever you go: "Always doing good and helping the poor." We all have labels that follow us, don't we? Labels have a way of walking closely behind us and showing up when we least expect them: loser, cheater, loner, underachiever, and more. Many times, we feel unable to escape labels put on us by ourselves and others. Sometimes it can feel impossible to shake a label, once tagged. However, if you were to have a label follow you everywhere, I think, "Always doing good and helping the poor," is a pretty solid one!

I wonder what the historians meant when they said she was "always doing good." I think they meant she was always doing good—not sometimes or often or when she felt like it. No, history records she was always doing good. But she did more than just do good; she helped the poor and others, looked out for the underdog, and stuck up for the least and the last. Tabitha was always rooting for the ones who didn't have a chance—the ones we always picked last in the neighborhood dodge ball game, the ones who didn't make the honor roll, the poor, the outcasts, and the ones labeled by society as never being able to measure up.

Unfortunately, the historical account of Tabitha takes a turn for the worst when records state that she suddenly fell ill and quickly and unexpectedly died (the proverbial good-guys-finish-last story). Panic set in. Her family, friends, and neighbors cried in disbelief and dismay as they held in their hands the robes and garments Tabitha made. They also held in their hearts a hope and a prayer for a miracle for this hero.

Legend tells us that a God-fearing apostle, Peter, heard of this tragedy and at once made his way to Joppa to see the beautiful gazelle, now lifeless. Without fanfare or drama in spite of the devastating scene, he spoke three commanding and powerful words of faith and hope amidst the fear and despair: "Tabitha, get up." It wasn't lengthy, drawn out, or overdone. It was quick, simple, and to the point. I like that.

Sometimes we don't need another long sermon, speech, lecture or mere political rhetoric. Sometimes what we need most are quick, powerful words of hope and destiny spoken to us, over us, and through us. And when we hear those words, we get up—we feel ourselves invigorated with new hope and purpose. That's exactly what Tabitha did. She got up and many people believed.

I don't really understand why she had to die in the first place. I don't necessarily like the fact that she had to die. It kind of makes the story a bit morbid, but I'm not the author of this fantastic story. Why would someone who went around always doing good have to be the one to die? If I had written the story, I certainly wouldn't have made another good guy die. Bad guys are supposed to die. But I do like the fact that in the face of death itself, there is hope and life.

Many people today are dead, though they live. They are living what I call the "unlived life." Yes, they're living . . . but not really. They're alive . . . but barely hanging on. They are the people of whom Henry David Thoreau wrote: "Most men live quiet lives of desperation and die with the song in them, living the 'unlived life.'"

I think what kept the beautiful gazelle alive was the inner conviction of purpose and destiny she had. Tabitha was on a mission of good. She lived for others and would not let even death stop her. She knew down deep that people were counting on her to come out of her sleep and rise up and continue to live a life of goodness.

When I first heard of Tabitha's story, it challenged and inspired me to live in her legacy. When I first heard about her and the life she lived, I determined that if others were to label me, I would be labeled "goodness" . . . as "someone who looked out for the unnoticed." Tabitha provoked me to be willing to overcome any and all obstacles, even death, to do good and help the poor. I hope she does the same for you.

Greatness, after all, in spite of its name, appears to be not so much a certain size as a certain quality in human lives. It may be present in lives whose range is very small.
(Phillips Brooks, 19th century clergyman)

Discovering Our Destiny, Like Mother Teresa

Whether you are like Mother Teresa or Tabitha, one of the keys you must discover is to uncover your personal mission of destiny. Every great leader who lived a life to do Good and be Great had a specific and detailed sense of purpose. For Mother Teresa, it was to look after and free the children of Calcutta and to be a voice for the poor. For Tabitha, it was to do good and care for the poor.

A few years ago I had the privilege of going to Honduras, in Central America, to deliver a container of food from the wonderful organization, Kids Against Hunger, that was 40' long by 10' wide and weighed several tons. It was an amazing trip and such a great joy for me to see packets of food assembled in Central Florida make it to that very poor country to help children and families that struggled with extreme poverty and hunger. I've been on hundreds of philanthropic missions in my life, but this experience was by far the most memorable for several reasons.

First was the effort and energy it took to get the food to the people who really needed it. The destination was at least three to four hours into the mountains, requiring the container to cross bridges, creeks, and canyons. Even as I write this it exhausts me just to recall the time and manpower it required. But after we delivered the food it was so rewarding to see the gratitude and appreciation on the faces of the children and their parents. It certainly made it worthwhile, and I'd do it again in a heartbeat.

The second memory I have of that trip was two days before we departed to return to Central Florida. One of the local missionary hosts mentioned in passing that the same town had an orphanage in it founded by Mother Teresa, and he wanted to know if we wanted to visit it. I've seen a lot of sites around the world, but I jumped at the opportunity to go and see that one. I'm glad I did. The experience was incredible. It was a first-class operation (as it should be): clean, maintained well, with friendly staff and volunteers. The experience was unforgettable. As I walked slowly through the halls, I couldn't help but think of the legacy Mother Teresa left to this community and the staff and volunteers. I felt the touch of compassion she instilled that is there even to this day.

Although Mother Teresa passed away several years ago, because of her life and passion, children rejected and neglected by their communities find a safe haven of acceptance. In that Honduran orphanage so far from Calcutta, the halls and rooms were filled with Mother Teresa's loving, caring heart that, in turn, touches the hearts of everyone who enters her campus of hope.

In Bill George's book, *True North*, he lists five dimensions of an authentic leader:

1. Pursuing purpose with passion.
2. Practicing solid values.
3. Leading with heart.
4. Establishing enduring relationships.
5. Demonstrating self-discipline.[5]

Please notice that the first key to becoming an authentic leader is pursuing purpose with passion. Every person who wants to live a beyond ordinary life must discover this key to help him or her live with purpose.[6]

9 Questions to Ask Yourself to Discover Your Destiny

1. *What makes you uniquely you?*
The reality is that no one can be authentic by trying to be like someone else. There is no doubt you can learn from others' experiences, but there is no way you can be successful trying to be like them. People trust you when you are genuine and authentic—not an imitation. As Dr. Reatha Clark King of General Mills said: "If you're aiming to be like somebody else, you're being a copycat because you think that's what people want you to do. You'll never be a star with that kind of thinking. But you might be a star—unreplicatable—by following your passion."

2. *What is your deepest desire?*
In order for you to uncover your purpose and destiny, you have to look within and ask yourself, "What is my deepest desire?" What keeps you up at night? What do you think about? What gives you the greatest joy? You see, those questions can only be answered by you. Your husband, wife, son,

daughter, boss, or friend cannot answer the deep questions about you that give you access into discovering your destiny. For some, this process may be painful and hard, but it is necessary to unlock your true potential.

3. What stirs passion inside you?

You can tell when you speak with someone when you strike what I call their "passion zone." It's that point in the conversation when their eyes light up, their face comes alive, and the volume in their voice increases. You can't fake this or force it. Your passion just bubbles up.

Recently, I spoke to a gifted international leader from South Africa, Delbert Groves. During our casual dinner conversation, the topic of mentoring young leaders suddenly arose, and Delbert's voice came alive, his eyes lit up, and the pace of his speech increased dramatically. As he spoke, I quickly observed we had hit his sweet spot of passion. It is much like drilling for oil. You know when you strike it, and when you do, there is no stopping it. It comes up quickly and suddenly and becomes obvious to all.

4. What flows out of you naturally?

When you are living and daily walking in your destiny, one of the first signs of this you will discover is that it functions and flows naturally within and from you. You will find that you don't have to work it up or try to manufacture it. It just seems to happen beautifully and naturally.

When I see other leaders flow in this gifting, I call it the "it factor." They have "it"—and it is noticeable and seemingly effortless. I'm certainly not saying that it doesn't take work and self-discipline, but when you discover your God-given destiny, you will not have to struggle or muster up the energy to do what is at hand. When the "it factor" is in effect, it is like breathing or walking; you don't have to think about it, it just happens naturally.

5. What produces the greatest results?

The fifth question you should ask yourself when you are evaluating your purpose and destiny is the question that many seem to overlook "What produces the greatest results?" This should be one of the questions you can quickly and confidently respond to when you investigate your past efforts. What are the events you can identify that have yielded the greatest results?

Many leadership training workshops and seminars will tell you to be balanced in all areas of leadership. They encourage leaders to master all the key levels of leadership. I find this approach will make you a "jack-of-all-trades . . . master of none," as the old saying goes. You have a very specific and detailed set of skills. Focus on these skills and master them. Don't try to be a "jack-of-all-trades." Look for and develop people around you who can complement you and assist you in your areas of weakness. This approach will help you stay focused on your gifting and also allow others who are gifted differently than you to flourish and mature. You will find that, as a team, you will be fulfilled and accomplish much because you are yielding the greatest results by focusing on your specific skill sets.

6. What qualities do others see in you?
Millions of dollars are spent each year on surveys and questionnaires by organizations all over the world. The knowledge and information these companies gather can be invaluable. As you ask yourself questions to help you uncover your purpose, one invaluable question is: "What qualities do others see in me?" If I were you (and I'm not), I suggest you take a few minutes to write down the names of ten people you trust and whose input you value. That's right: Write down the names of ten people from your work, family, friends, church, or community, who will give you priceless information about you, for free.

10 People Who Will Help Me See the Questions I May Not See

1.
2.
3.
4.
5.
6.

7.

8.

9.

10.

When you complete the list, simply email the ten people and ask what each sees in you.

This may seem a bit awkward and uncomfortable for you, but be assured your closest friends would be honored to assist you. They will be the most helpful in identifying the qualities in you that are noticeable and obvious to everyone around you. When you do this little project, you will immediately see what is so obvious to others. Their comments and observations will not only encourage you, but also help you identify the skills and gifts within you.

Remember, as you evaluate your gifts, what you see in the "gift mirror" when you look at yourself may not be what others see in you. This small but powerful project will inspire you to assimilate what's really in you and what others also see.

7. *What dreams are impossible for you to ignore?*

I don't know about you, but it seems like the older I get the more enjoyable sleep time gets. When I was younger, you couldn't get me to lie down for five minutes; but as I approach fifty-four years of age, give me five minutes of rest and I'll take it every time. When you lie down to sleep, what are the dreams in you that are impossible to ignore? I'm asking you again to take a few minutes and list five dreams you have that you cannot overlook.

Dreams I Cannot Ignore:

1.

2.

3.

4.

5.

These dreams, goals, and visions have been given to you—only you. You may be the only person in eight billion people on earth who has these dreams, goals, and visions right now. You may be the only one in the world who can see them fulfilled. These cannot be taken lightly—or for granted. They have been placed in you for a purpose, and failure to believe in your dreams and act on them can ultimately disqualify you from seeing them accomplished. Unfortunately, others who are responsible—who do not ignore their dreams but act on them—may inherit yours if you do not act first. Let's be determined not to let others fulfill our dreams because we overlooked them and did not take them seriously.

8. What is the little voice inside of you saying?
Be careful on this one. If you and I go around telling people we hear voices, they may try and lock us up for a few years. This may sound a bit crazy, but I believe that each of us has a "little voice" inside of us to help us stay on track, and that guides us as we walk through life. Because of my personal faith, I personally believe this voice is the Holy Spirit who has been given by God to those who believe.

Some say this voice is their conscience; others identify it with different terms. The purpose of this is not to try to convert you or persuade you to believe as I do, but to simply make you aware that there is a power available to you. This voice may be small, but it is very powerful and influential. This voice will be your best counselor, guide, and navigator as you walk through the very confusing and complicated journey called life. Don't try to walk this journey alone. It's too risky and too much is at stake. Trust your voice within to help you identify the destiny in you.

9. What patterns keep repeating in you?
Life is a series of seasons that keep repeating themselves year after year. Just as in the natural seasons, where we have spring, summer, fall, and winter, we have seasons in life. These are patterns we can discover that keep reoccurring year after year. Pay careful attention to these patterns in your life. These patterns may unlock valuable details that can assist you in discovering your destiny. These patterns can be both helpful and

harmful, so identifying them accurately can assist you greatly in your move forward.

Howard Schultz, the chairman and CEO of Starbucks, started his career at Xerox but felt the environment was too bureaucratic and rigid for him to flourish. While others thrived in the Xerox culture, Schultz yearned to go his own way. "I had to find a place where I could be myself," he said. "I could not settle for anything less. You must have the courage to follow an unconventional path. You can't value or measure your life experience in the moment, because you never know when you're going to find the true path that enables you to find your voice. The reservoir of all my life experiences shaped me as a person and a leader."[8]

Questions for you on ....
Chapter 2: Discover Your Destiny To Do Good, Be Great

1. When you read about Mother Teresa, what are some of the do good be great qualities you see?

2. Pick out one of the quotes from Mother Teresa and discuss why this particular quote inspires you.

3. What attributes do Mother Teresa and Tabitha have in common? Explain.

4. When you hear the phrase, "discovering your destiny," what does that mean to you?

5. What is your specific destiny and what in the world are you here for?

6. What is your "it" factor? What attributes and characteristics make you uniquely you?

Notes

Great Quotes from a Great Leader
Bono

- *"Where you live in the world should not determine whether you live in the world."*
- *"When you truly accept that those children in some far off place in the global village have the same value as you in God's eyes or even in just your eyes, then your life is forever changed; you see something that you can't un-see."*
- *"Poverty breeds despair. We know this. Despair breeds violence. We know this. In turbulent times, isn't it cheaper, and smarter, to make friends out of potential enemies than to defend yourself against them later?"*
- *"Actually, oddly enough, I think my work—the activism—will be forgotten. And I hope it will. Because I hope those problems will have gone away."*
- *"I truly believe that when the history books are written, our age will be remembered for three things: the war on terror, the digital revolution, and what we did—or did not do—to put the fire out in Africa. History, like God, is watching what we do."*
- *"Music can change the world because it can change people."*
- *"Stop asking God to bless what you're doing. Find out what God's doing. It's already blessed."*
- *"Whenever I see grace, I'm moved."*
- *"To be one, to be united is a great thing. But to respect the right to be different is maybe even greater."*
- *"When you align yourself with God's purpose as described in the Scriptures, something special happens to your life."*

3

Camping Out in the Land Called Good

*KEY 3: BEYOND ORDINARY PEOPLE WALK THE
ROAD LESS TRAVELED WITH A DISSATISFACTION
OF STATUS QUO*

BONO—Do Good, Be Great for Those Battling World Hunger

As the revered front man for U2, the massively popular Irish rock band, Bono has filled entertainment arenas across the globe for more than thirty years. On the world's political stage, though, the Grammy-winning lead singer is also highly respected for a different reason. Heads of state across the globe recognize him for being a keen, persuasive, and influential crusader for economic justice on behalf of the world's poor.

Cofounder of humanitarian organizations such as DATA and the ONE Campaign, Bono has shown he can successfully unite the entertainment and political arenas in his effort to do Good, and be Great. He has a long held commitment to social justice that reflects a passion he credits chiefly to his Christian beliefs.

His activism began in earnest in 1983 when he accepted an invitation from Irish Prime Minister Garrett Fitzgerald to join the Select Government Action Committee on Unemployment. Two years later, he traveled with his wife, Alison, to Ethiopia to work in a feeding camp with Christian charity World Vision. At that time, during a visit to El Salvador, he witnessed a military attack on a village, later expressing the experience musically on the Grammy-winning U2 album, *The Joshua Tree.*

Since the turn of the new century, Bono has rallied entertainment and political figures alike to lobby for forgiveness of Third World debt. In 2002, he established the nonprofit advocacy group DATA (Debt, Aid, Trade for Africa) in a continuing effort to aid the world's most impoverished and threatened populations. In 2004, he launched The ONE Campaign to raise awareness of global poverty and to change governmental policies in areas such as aid, trade, and justice. In 2005, the Make Poverty History campaign was launched. It comprises coalitions of NGOs, faith groups, and individuals working to end extreme poverty. All three campaigns have the goal of ending AIDS and extreme poverty in Africa.

Bono was equally key in performing in and helping to organize the Live 8 concerts in 2005—a series of events across the globe designed to pressure world leaders to increase aid, cancel Third World debt, and improve trade agreements with the world's poorest countries.

Bono's international influence is a by-product of his musical stardom, which grew fairly quickly, but not before he endured a rocky upbringing in Ireland.

He was born Paul David Hewson on May 10, 1960, in Dublin—the second child of Brendan and Iris Hewson, who were Catholic and Protestant, respectively. Theirs was an unusual unity of faith for parents at a time when Ireland was deeply divided over religion, and Protestants and Catholics engaged in often deadly clashes.

At age fourteen, Paul suffered a devastating loss when his mother died of a brain hemorrhage while attending her father's funeral. His home life immediately turned traumatic. Paul and his father did not get along well and would never enjoy a close relationship. He has said that his father's belief, "To dream is to be disappointed," became the fuel for his own passion to dream big and pursue his dreams.

Originally he wanted to be an actor. He seemed, instead, to find his creative niche when he landed the role of lead singer of a band formed with his high school mates, Larry Mullen Jr., David Evans (later nicknamed

"The Edge"), and Adam Clayton. They called themselves Feedback, then Hype, and finally, U2.

Bono, Edge, and Larry had become Christians, and soon after the formation of the band, they became involved in the Dublin-based non-denominational group, Shalom. Eventually feeling pressured by Shalom's leaders to choose between rock music and Jesus, U2 and Shalom parted ways. Since then, Bono's Christian faith has played a major role in his life, though largely apart from mainstream Christian churches. Today the band has been awarded twenty-two Grammys and thirteen gold or platinum records.

Along the way, Bono has attempted to distance himself from the "pop star" persona that has followed him. He has even been known to invite fans into his home near Dublin. A father and family man, he married his childhood sweetheart, Alison Stewart, in 1982, and the couple has raised four children.

Apart from the band, Bono has continued to appear on world stages as part of celebrity gatherings and musical events supporting relief and humanitarian causes. In 2003, he was awarded the King Center Humanitarian Award by Coretta Scott King, widow of Dr. Martin Luther King Jr. He also met in Rome with Pope John Paul II to discuss ways to ease the financial strain of poor nations. He has been invited to address the US Congress as well as legislative bodies in Europe.

In 2004, he was a guest speaker at the University of Pennsylvania commencement ceremony where he challenged the Ivy League graduates to get involved in fighting the AIDS epidemic in Africa. In 2006, Bono co-founded (RED), a division of the ONE Campaign. It seeks to persuade companies with global brands to sell product lines from which a portion of the profits will be donated to fighting AIDS, tuberculosis, and malaria.

He has even created his own socially conscious clothing line, EDUN, along with Alison and fashion designer Rogan Gregory. EDUN seeks to promote fair trade and sustainable growth by basing production in poor communities. Workers are encouraged to use their skills in an environmentally friendly way to create garments that can be sold at a fair price.

When challenging his fellow Christians to involvement in efforts to end poverty, economic injustice, and AIDS, Bono has said: "Distance does not decide who is your brother and who is not. The church is going to have to become the conscience of the free market if it's to have any meaning in this world—and stop being its apologist."

Bono's energy and commitment to do Good, be Great have earned him numerous honors, including a knighthood in Britain, the Légion d'honneur in France, and two nominations for the Nobel Peace Prize.

Creating a Legacy of Do Good, Be Great

I so admire the life and legacy of Bono. He is one person I would love to spend the day with to ask him how he developed such an incredible passion to do Good, and be Great. I bet he learned those traits at an early age. I bet his parents raised him in an atmosphere in which he could develop and nurture the qualities that make him the person he is today.

As a father, I also want to create an atmosphere in which my children can believe they too can live a life beyond ordinary—a life of not only doing good, but also to do Good, and be Great.

Each day before getting all four children off to school, the routine went like this:

1. Clothes on . . . *check.*
2. Breakfast done . . . *check.*
3. Homework completed . . . *check.*
4. Lunch in backpack . . . *check.*
5. Backpack on back . . . *check.*

Often it was a flurry of activity and pandemonium—juice boxes flying all over the kitchen, Goldfish crackers flung from box to bag, and peanut butter and jelly slapped on bread quickly (but precisely). The goal was to get all four kids into the SUV without losing my temper, or without one of them losing their life!

It was only a few minutes' ride to Dommerich, the Maitland, Florida, elementary school they attended. It didn't matter that the drive was a short one or how crazy things got while preparing my kids and loading them in the car; on the way I always made it a point to leave them with a challenge and a charge before they hopped out and made their way to class. I would look each one of them in the eye and say, "Do good today."

My intentions were pure and my heart was right. Still, if I had it to do all over again—and hopefully I will one day with my grandchildren—I would add a bit of a twist to my admonition. (That's the beauty of having grandkids—you get another chance to redo things!) Instead of simply saying, "Do good," I would add: "Do Good, be *Great*."

It's a small adjustment to the wording, but it makes all the difference in the world. Most people want to do good, but if we truly are going to make a lasting difference in our children, families, community, nation, and world, then we have to move from Good to Great. It is important that we make the leap from average to *beyond ordinary*; from doing good, to do Good, be Great.

I'm afraid that instead of do Good, be Great in our churches, families, nonprofits, and companies, we've made the decision to camp out in the land called "good."

Camping Out in the Land Called Good

I don't like camping much. I love the outdoors—the fires, walks in the wilderness, and fun around the campground. But I guess one reason I don't like camping is all the effort it requires. It takes a lot of work to pack all the gear and equipment into the car—the tents, cooking gear, flashlights, bug spray, backpacks, and sleeping bags. It's a ton of work for only a few days. Then, guess what's next? You do it all over again. You have to break down camp and load the stuff back into the car. Don't forget that when you get all the stuff home, you have to clean it, air it out, repack it, and store it in your garage for the next adventure. My point is, if you go through all that trouble to have a camping experience, then *really* camp out and don't hold back.

Don't go for a few hours or a day or two—go big. Stay a week, two weeks, a month. Make your experience worth the effort. Explore and venture out. Move beyond the yard chair and the fire pit and see nature at its best.

When it comes to doing good, I think many of us view it the way I look at camping. We have made a decision to camp out in the land called good. By that I mean, we seem to be content with just doing good, but not with truly venturing out into the land that's great. We do just enough to get by. We have settled in and believe we have arrived. In reality, there is more for us to experience and explore.

When it comes to helping resolve the issues of world hunger, poverty, domestic violence, or Third World injustice, we have to be convinced that our efforts and intentions of doing good are good enough. It's healthy to examine our efforts both locally and internationally, evaluate our good works, and see if we can move beyond the land of good into the land to do good, be Great, where we become more productive and effective in our efforts to cure cancer, eliminate hunger, or erase poverty. I think it's interesting that the old saying, "The road to hell is paved with good intentions," is really addressing those who want to camp out in the land of good, telling them: "Do more and do it well."

A Very Good Example of Do Good, Be Great

Before we move ahead, I have to warn you: Many of you know that in addition to being a speaker and nonprofit leader, I'm a minister. For the past thirty years, I have taken my occupation as a minister into the world of compassion and philanthropy. My life's mission is to love God and to love others. I don't want to just hang out in the church building; I want to live my faith out in our world. Along with a wonderful staff, I have done just that in downtown Orlando, Florida, helping thousands of families each month with food assistance, medical care, social services, and so much more. My faith motivates me to do this.

In this book, I will be sharing from my faith and my experiences. Understand I am not trying to be preachy, religious, or self-righteous.

At times I will use the Bible as a reference, which is by the way, both the most popular and best-selling book of all time. Don't get caught up in this minor detail. Don't let it be a deal breaker. I will use many quotes, stories, and references, including the Bible. Don't get hung up on it. Learn from it, take its principles, and apply them to your life. I'm confident its words will inspire, challenge, and motivate you as they have me.

The Jewish culture tells us of a man who was not willing just to do good. He was committed to do Good, be Great. His passion was not to camp out in the land called good and live an ordinary life. Rather, He was passionate about doing Good in a Great way.

The Bible records this verse to help us see the power of moving beyond normal good works to exceptional philanthropy and efforts that yield lasting results: *"You know what has happened . . . how God anointed Jesus of Nazareth with the Holy Spirit and power, and how he went around doing good and healing all who were under the power of the devil, because God was with him"* (Acts 10:38, NIV).

I absolutely love that passage of Scripture. In just thirty-three words, it completely and accurately describes the passion of moving from good to Great when helping people who are perplexed and in need. There are a few things in the verse that I want to bring to your attention.

1. God gifted Jesus with the power and ability to do Good .

There is a special grace, gift, or ability to do Good, and be Great that I believe we all possess. I call it the "it factor." You've seen this principle in action just like I have. You see it in someone who possesses talents and abilities that are not manufactured or worked up. Their gift just flows and it's a joy to sit back and watch these types of people in action. They are naturals, and what they do appears to be effortless.

You can have that same gifting. It is not set apart for a special few. I believe each of us possesses that unique and authentic gift. It is inside each and every one of us. We all need to be reminded that in our world, people who are hungry, children who are desperate, families that are hopeless—all are counting on you and me to have a special gifting that will help them and others and bring hope to a hurting world.

2. Jesus, our Do Good, Be Great example, went around doing Good.

Wow, what an amazing statement! Jesus went around "doing Good." Let's stop right there for a moment. He went around doing Good. I love that. He was a natural at doing Good. His life's mission was to live a life of doing Good—and not just doing Good, but to do Good, and be Great. The word *Good* in this verse has a very interesting meaning. The original Greek word is *eergeto*, pronounced *yoo-erg-et-eh-o*.

Now, I'm not a Greek scholar, so don't try to get me to say this for you, but just by looking at this word I have a feeling its meaning is pretty significant. Any word pronounced *yoo-erg-et-eh-o* has to be special. Stop just for a moment and try to say it. It means, "to be philanthropic, a worker of good."

Jesus was one of the very first philanthropists. I don't know about you, but whenever I think of philanthropists I certainly do not think of Jesus. Many of us think of Andrew Carnegie or John D. Rockefeller, but not Jesus. When I think of philanthropists, I think of wealthy people dressed in tuxedos and expensive dresses going to fancy ballrooms in expensive cars, sipping expensive wines, engaging in eloquent conversations, and at the end of the evening, throwing a few thousand dollars at a silent auction for a another fun trip (though, most importantly, for the tax deduction).

Even though the word *philanthropic* sounds sophisticated and stuffy, we are mandated to go around everywhere, every day to everyone, and do good.

John Wesley was the ultimate philanthropist and man of compassion and passion for the poor. I admire his work greatly. The United Methodist denomination and the world have benefited greatly from his vision and leadership. I love one quote of his in particular. In fact, I include it at the bottom of each email I send from my church. I hope that over many years,

I will send out tens of thousands of emails with this message of inspiration and conviction to do Good, and be Great: *"Do all the good you can, by all the means you can, in all the ways you can, in all the places you can, at all the times you can, to all the people you can, as long as you can"* (John Wesley).

I guess you could call Jesus, John Wesley, and all the other philanthropists in the world—including you and me—*do-gooders*. Just like Tabitha in chapter one, each of us—by "always doing good" in the same way that Jesus "went around doing good"—can follow in their steps and live a life of do Good, be Great.

3. Jesus healed all those who were hurting.

That's an incredible verse. And it is here we move from good to Great. Jesus wasn't content just with doing good. He wasn't satisfied with camping out in the land called good. He realized that good wasn't good enough. He knew that His good had to move to Great and He healed people who were under the power of the devil.

Millions of people live under a curse. Poverty and hunger and injustice are rampant; they are at an all-time high. Never before in history have we had so much innovation and technology, yet so much hurt and pain at the same time.

The word *healed* in Greek is *iaomai*, pronounced *ee-AH-om-ahee*. It is a verb meaning, "to cure, make whole." Let that sink in for a moment. The first step is to do Good. The second step is to make whole. The premise of this book—*Do Good, Be Great*—is to inspire and motivate you to execute both Good and Great by doing good *and* making whole.

The One-Two Punch to Do Good, Be Great

I've never been much of a fighter. I think my only fight was in the eighth grade, with a dear friend, Blake Thomas, when we both attended Lee Junior High School in Orlando. If my memory serves me correctly, we got off the bus and started fighting. We fought for no apparent reason. It was just testosterone flowing and kids being kids.

He grabbed me by the neck, so I did the same to him, and for about five minutes, we were there moving from side to side, groaning and yelling, but not doing much punching. After about five minutes we let go, said goodbye, and moved on. If I had known what I know now, I would have "in love" thrown the one punch. You get it: jab right, then go left with a quick uppercut. Swift and effective, this is called the one-two punch.

In Acts 10:38 (NIV), we are given the one-two punch of effective charity: *yoo-erg-et-eh-o* and *ee-AH-om-ahee*; *"doing good"* and *"making whole."*

I'm afraid we've been fighting poverty without seeing any results: A lot of activity, funds, and movement, but little outcome (in other words, a lot of *yoo-erg-et-eh-o* and no *ee-AH-om-ahee*; a lot of doing good, but little making whole). Our churches, communities, and world need more one-two punchers—more people wanting a do Good, be Great attitude. We need fewer people who are willing to live in the land called good and more who want to see hurt, wounded, and impoverished people healed and made whole.

We can give away food for the rest of our lives to families in need, and guess what? Next week, they will be back—still in need. Believe me, if they are showing up at your charity or church asking for help, it means they've been to every other one asking for the same thing. They will be back for more.

Doing good is not our answer. We have to do Good, be Great. We need to help, and then make whole. Let's choose to be one-two punchers in our fight against poverty. Hopefully, we will knock out injustice, hunger, and suffering with an effective right jab and left uppercut.

One of the unique qualities Bono and Jesus share is their amazing dissatisfaction with the status quo. I really believe one key to living a beyond ordinary life is not being content with the way things are. We must be driven so that we push the envelope in every area of our lives and are not content with camping out in the land called good. Let's look at what it takes to fight complacency, apathy, excuses, fear, bad habits, comfort, and isolation.

The Key to Living Beyond Ordinary: Dissatisfaction with the Status Quo

If there is dissatisfaction with the status quo, good. If there is ferment, so much the better. If there is restlessness, I am pleased. Then let there be ideas, and hard thought, and hard work. If man feels small, let man make himself bigger. (Hubert H. Humphrey)

Status Quo's (Best) Friends

Status quo has many friends. They have similar tastes, and they share common beliefs and values.

Friend #1—Complacency

The first friend of status quo is complacency. Complacency likes life the way it is. It sees no need to change or better itself. It is content and most satisfied when life is constant and predictable. Complacency prides itself on avoiding risks and challenges. When complacency hears from others, "You haven't changed a bit," it takes that as the ultimate compliment.

Those who desire to do Good, be Great and live beyond ordinary will try at all costs to avoid this subtle yet powerful friend called complacency.

Friend #2—Excuses

Many people these days carry with them in their back pocket or purse a very lethal weapon. They use it every day. This handy instrument quickly comes out when they face responsibility, accountability, or personal ownership. Many people whip the weapon out to defend themselves any time someone questions them about or confronts them with change, the need to move forward, or living beyond ordinary.

This effective little weapon is also a friend of status quo's. It is called "excuses." So many people these days carry excuses with them without realizing it keeps them down, unmotivated, and unaccountable. This friend is so subtle and clever—it slips out every day to keep people immobilized, even paralyzed.

Here are a few comebacks Excuses provides for people who are content with living ordinary lives and don't want to move forward into do Good, be Great. Maybe you identify with these and can even add to this toxic list. I call them the "It will . . ."; "I'm too . . . "; "What if . . . "; "I don't . . . "; "It's just . . . "; and "I'll do it . . ." excuses.

It will . . .
— take too long
— never happen
— require too much
— cost too much
— be too difficult

I'm too . . .
— old
— young
— poor
— dumb
— set in my ways

What if . . .
— it doesn't work
— we don't succeed
— we are wrong
— we fail
— we have to start again

I don't . . .
— think it will work
— know if we can do it
— believe we can succeed
— see another way

It's just . . .
— too complicated
— too hard
— too complex
— too messy

I'll do it . . .
— tomorrow
— when the kids move out
— when the timing is right
— when the stars line up

Friend #3—Fear

This may be Status Quo's greatest ally, partner, and friend. But he is probably our worst enemy.

Fear is one of the most hideous foes to those desirous to do Good, be Great. Everyone who has discovered the joy of living beyond ordinary has faced this enemy and learned to conquer it daily. On any given day, fear keeps hundreds of millions of people entrapped and immobilized.

There is an old biblical story of a man named Job who had it all. He had money, fame, power, and a beautiful family. On the surface, he had it all. But under the surface there was a small and deadly cancer called fear that gripped his life. You couldn't tell from his outer appearance that he was battling this opponent. Inside, though, was a man wasting away from fear, and he was eventually overcome by it.

One day, Job lost it all—his family, his business, his retirement, his IRA, and his pension—in one day. In the aftermath of his terrible personal disaster, Job's response was, *"For the thing which I greatly feared is come upon me,"* (Job 3:25, KJV). Job was so gripped by this enemy called fear that he actually attracted this force into his life. Here is an incredible principle for those who desire to live beyond ordinary lives: *You attract what you focus on.*

Job was secretly focused on the fear of losing his empire and he was spot-on when he said, *"What I dreaded (focused on) has happened to me"* (Job 3:25, NIV, parentheses added). Be careful what you focus on because it will be brought into your life by the power of fear.

I really believe that when you focus your energy on sickness, tragedy, financial disaster, broken relationships, or foolish living, you will attract that to your life. The great news is that another power, one opposite to fear, is available to you and me; it's called faith.

Faith is more powerful than fear. When you decide to live the beyond ordinary life, you allow faith to be your source of strength, not fear. This certainly doesn't mean you don't (or won't) have fears. It means that you determine to set your heart on faith instead of fear. I'm personally inspired and motivated by the biblical verse, *"The just shall live by faith"* (Romans 1:17, KJV).

Make it a point today to overcome your personal fears and "live by faith," as the verse says. Fear and worry will always be around to try to keep you focused on all the bad in the world and all the negative stuff that can happen. Be determined instead to live by faith and you will see this force come alive in you and defeat that enemy we call fear.

Over the years I have noticed several fears that constantly keep people imprisoned or immobile. In the following section I list a few of them and then give you the opportunity to list a few of your own that could be holding you back from do Good, be Great.

5 Common Fears That Keep People From Living Beyond Ordinary

1. Fear of failure
2. Fear of the unknown
3. Fear of rejection
4. Fear of disaster
5. Fear of the future

List five fears you face:

1.
2.

3.
4.
5.

In Dr. David Jeremiah's book, *What Are You Afraid Of?*, he identifies ten of life's greatest and most common fears:

1. **Disaster:** Fear of natural calamity
2. **Disease:** Fear of serious illness
3. **Debt:** Fear of financial collapses
4. **Defeat:** Fear of failure
5. **Disconnection:** Fear of being alone
6. **Disapproval:** Fear of Rejection
7. **Danger:** Fear of sudden trouble
8. **Depression:** Fear of mental breakdown
9. **Death:** Fear of dying
10. **Deity:** Fear of God [9]

Friend #4—Bad Habits

Bad Habits can keep you from living in the land called great, forever. If you ever want to break out of normalcy, you will have to both identify and conquer the bad habits that keep you from living your potential; bad habits such as being late to meetings or appointments, not returning phone calls or emails promptly, watching too much TV, or not exercising on a regular basis.

Here's a short list of good habits that will assist you to do Good, and be Great. By mastering these good habits, like taking the time to personally write Thank You notes to people in your life or remembering your friends' birthdays and anniversaries, you will position yourself to break free from status quo living.

1. The habit of **Listening**
2. The habit of **Thanking**
3. The habit of **Learning**
4. The habit of **Going the Extra Mile**

5. The habit of **Taking Calculated Risks**
6. The habit of **Forgiving**
7. The habit of **Personal Responsibility**
8. The habit of **Giving Grace**
9. The habit of **Flexibility**

Friend #5—Comfort

I absolutely love the following statement encouraging boys to move boldly into manhood. Although it was originally written to boys and men, I believe its principles apply to anyone. As you read this, let it inspire you to break free of comfort and motivate you to move beyond ordinary:

Manhood

"The World Needs Men"

- *who cannot be bought;*
- *whose word is their bond;*
- *who put character above wealth;*
- *who are larger than their vocations;*
- *who do not hesitate to take chances;*
- *who will not lose their identity in a crowd;*
- *who will be as honest in small things as in great things;*
- *who will make no compromise with wrong;*
- *whose ambitions are not confined to their own selfish desires;*
- *who will not say they do it "because everybody else does it";*
- *who are true to their friends through good report and evil report, in adversity as well as in prosperity;*
- *who do not believe that shrewdness and cunning are the best qualities for winning success;*
- *who are not ashamed to stand for the truth when it is unpopular;*
- *who can say "no" with emphasis, although the rest of the world says, "yes."* [10]

God, make me this kind of man. (Leonard Wagner)

Friend #6—Isolation

The sixth friend of status quo is one I call isolation. There will be times in your life when this enemy will try to get you alone, where you become vulnerable.

There is power in numbers and relationships. There are people around you whom you need, and they need you. Often, however, we get discouraged, start to feel defeated, and then withdraw from the very ones we need to be around. Try with all your power to avoid isolation. It is your enemy and not your friend because it seeks to pull you away from your sources of strength and encouragement.

I recently completed a three-day safari in Zambia, in the southern part of Africa. I had the privilege of fulfilling this bucket list item of mine with three dear friends whom I admire and respect greatly. Whenever I have new adventures and experiences, I always look beyond the natural events for the supernatural "life lessons" in each one. Every day is filled with these lessons that can help you to be a better husband, wife, father, mother, or leader. One day in the South Luangwa National Park was no exception.

The nighttime safari started at 4 p.m. As we loaded the Range Rover, we were full of expectation and excitement. After several minutes, our tour guide drove up on a pack of four wild dogs. I didn't think much of it until after a few minutes, when I saw there were four other tours following the pack of dogs. The guides knew what we didn't know at the time: they had stumbled upon the pack at the right time. It was time for a hunt.

The pack seemed tired and desperate, but very strategic and calculated. They would walk seemingly without a plan; but boy, was I wrong about that. Suddenly they would stop; their ears erect, and instantly focus on their prey. Without hesitation, each would slip into its role and position within the pack, and together they would effortlessly stalk a group of zebras or antelope.

The guide provided us with minute-by-minute instruction and, without knowing it, also gave me incredible insight and a valuable life lesson. He said the pack looks for and senses a weak, young, or isolated victim. Instantly, the safari had a deeper meaning and purpose for me. I began to notice the precision and tactical positioning of the dogs as they strategically focused on the animal that was isolated.

We followed the pack for a while and watched them make several attempts and runs at the prey. We left them to view elephants, hippos, giraffes, and dozens of other beautiful animals. As we did, I wondered if the dogs were successful in their hunt.

At 7:45 p.m., as we left the park, we happened to come upon the dogs and saw that, in fact, they had been successful. They were enjoying a night of rest in the open range with a belly full of food and another day a few hours away.

May this safari life lesson serve as an example for us all. When we are tempted to isolate ourselves and pull away from our trusted friends and colleagues, let's remind ourselves of this simple yet powerful story. May we let it encourage us to avoid isolation and stay clear of the roving pack.

The only thing necessary for the triumph of evil is for good men to do nothing. (Edmund Burke)

Questions for you on ....
Chapter 3: Camping Out in the Land Called Good

1. When you read about Bono, what are some of the do good be great qualities you see?

2. Pick out one of the quotes from Bono and discuss why this particular quote inspires you.

3. Have you ever camped out in a land called good? If so, what does it look like, feel like and how do you feel living there?

4. Jesus was described as one who "went around doing good and healing all who were oppressed. What does that mean to you and how can you follow in this legacy?

5. What are 5 things you can begin doing right now that can break the "status quo" living?

6. What 5 excuses have you used lately to justify your average living and how can you begin to change from good to great?

Notes

Great Quotes from a Great Leader
Nelson Mandela

- *"Overcoming poverty is not a task of charity, it is an act of justice. Like slavery and apartheid, poverty is not natural. It is man-made and it can be overcome and eradicated by the actions of human beings. Sometimes it falls on a generation to be great. YOU can be that great generation. Let your greatness blossom."*
- *"To deny people their human rights is to challenge their very humanity."*
- *"There can be no keener revelation of a society's soul than the way in which it treats its children."*
- *"Our human compassion binds us the one to the other—not in pity or patronizingly, but as human beings who have learnt how to turn our common suffering into hope for the future."*
- *"I am fundamentally an optimist. Whether that comes from nature or nurture, I cannot say. Part of being optimistic is keeping one's head pointed toward the sun, one's feet moving forward. There were many dark moments when my faith in humanity was sorely tested, but I would not and could not give myself up to despair. That way lays defeat and death."*
- *"When a man is denied the right to live the life he believes in, he has no choice but to become an outlaw."*
- *"It always seems impossible until it's done."*
- *"While poverty persists, there is no true freedom."*
- *"And as we let our own light shine, we unconsciously give other people permission to do the same"*

4

When Goodness Isn't Good Enough

KEY 4: BEYOND ORDINARY PEOPLE
CONTINUALLY LIVE LIFE IN SEARCH OF EXCELLENCE

NELSON MANDELA—Do Good, Be Great for Those Oppressed

E arly in 1990, President F.W. de Klerk of South Africa stunned the world when he announced that a "time for negotiation" with the country's black opposition leaders had come. For more than half a century, the wall of apartheid had separated blacks and whites in South Africa. Now it was teetering, and de Klerk, a white Afrikaner, was about to give it a final push.

The shock waves of his stunning declaration rippled outward after he went on to say that all legal restrictions would be lifted on more than thirty banned organizations, including the militant African National Congress and the South African Communist Party. Capital punishment would be suspended, he stated, and political prisoners not convicted of any violent activity would be released. It was a stunning, transformative moment that black South Africans had prayed for decades to see.

Unseen by the world at the time were the series of secret meetings that had begun in December 1989 between an unlikely duo: President de Klerk and inmate Nelson Mandela—the internationally known figurehead of the black opposition who had been jailed for the previous twenty-seven years after being convicted of conspiracy to overthrow the government.

What emerged from their discussions was nothing short of a miraculous, nonviolent transformation of a nation.

Within ninety days, Mandela was released from prison. Within three years, the two men were co-recipients of the Nobel Peace Prize, awarded to them for their efforts to heal their deeply divided nation.

Most astounding, however, was that in less than ten years, Mandela went on to lead the emancipation of South Africa from apartheid, serve as the nation's first black president, and become a global emblem of forgiveness and reconciliation. His legacy as a leader who did good, Great is unquestioned. And his journey from the son of African royalty to prisoner of the state to chief executive of the state is the stuff of which miracles are made.

Nelson was born Rolihlahla Dahlibunga Mandela on July 18, 1918, in Mwezo village, the traditional home of the Thembu people. His parents were Thembu, a tribal group of the Xhosa nation. His father was of royal blood and an adviser to the Thembu chiefs. His mother was a Christian and she had her son baptized at the local Methodist church. Mandela received his primary education at a Methodist mission, where he took the name Nelson.

As a young man practicing law in the Soweto area of Johannesburg, he was involved in anti-colonial politics and joined the African National Congress (ANC). The ANC was the foremost antiapartheid movement in the country.

Apartheid, which means "apartness," had been entrenched since 1948, when the white population, a 14 percent minority, ensured that the Nationalist Party would hold political power for the next forty-five years in the nation. The doctrine was designed to secure their control over the rest of the population. Under apartheid, blacks were banned from politics, living in white areas, and attending white government schools. Interracial marriage was illegal. Land acts required blacks to live in *bantustans* ("homelands"), and whites controlled 87 percent of the total land area.

Mandela pursued social change, nonviolently at first. But in 1961, a year after police killed sixty-nine peaceful demonstrators in Sharpeville township, he led the ANC in armed insurrection against the government. Mandela was arrested and charged with sabotage and conspiracy to overthrow the state—each a capital crime. During his trial, he stated his personal convictions in open court. It had a prophetic ring, when set against the backdrop of his personal history as one who would decades later peacefully liberate his country from apartheid.

"I have fought against white domination, and I have fought against black domination," Mandela told the court. "I have cherished the ideal of a democratic and free society in which all persons will live together in harmony and with equal opportunities. It is an ideal for which I hope to live and to see realized."

He was sentenced to life in prison at age forty-four and put on a ferry to Robben Island, a maximum security facility about seven miles out to sea, off Cape Town. Two-and-a-half decades later, Mandela emerged from prison a different person. He exuded forgiveness, not militancy. He told the Rev. Michael Cassidy, an Anglican clergyman, that he had been deeply impressed by Billy Graham's sermons, which he watched on the prison television. Reportedly, he made a Christian commitment after watching a Graham crusade, and wrote to the evangelist's ministry to tell them about his decision.

In April 1994, during South Africa's first democratic elections and only four years after his release from prison, Mandela won the presidency by a landslide. He was inaugurated on May 10, 1994, with de Klerk as his first deputy. On May 14th, he made his inaugural speech before an audience that never expected to see the deep-seated culture of apartheid end without civil war. It was a remarkable moment of transition in a nation so polarized by race.

As president from 1994 to 1999, Mandela devoted himself to moderating the bitterness of his black electorate and reassuring whites who feared reprisals from his government. Amazingly, he instituted a commission to provide amnesty to apartheid enforcers, telling parliament he was persuaded reconciliation would "further consolidate nation-building." More than three thousand people applied for amnesty. Justifying his actions in an interview with the *New York Times* in 2007, Mandela said, "Leaders cannot afford to hate."

Desmond Tutu, the former Anglican archbishop of Cape Town, has noted that without Mandela, South Africa easily could have descended into civil war. "Had Nelson Mandela . . . not been willing to forgive," Tutu said, "we would not have even reached first base." By that he meant the reconciliation of a divided South Africa, practically overnight, through a peaceful democratic vote instead of with war and violent revenge.

Today, history remembers Nelson Mandela as one who exemplified a spirit of excellence in his efforts to bring good to the people around him. Truly it can be said that he lived a life beyond ordinary. He demonstrated that, to do good, be Great, it is possible not only to change our neighborhoods and communities, but also to transform a nation.

Mandela lived to the age of ninety-five and died at his home in Johannesburg on December 5, 2013.

It's no mistake that this chapter highlights the life and legacy of Nelson Mandela. As I write it, I happen to be in the southern African country of Zambia, very close to South Africa, where Mandela left his imprint for hope, change, and of living a life of excellence. His influence extended beyond South Africa, even around the world. I witnessed this during my trip to Africa, when I was asked to address leaders in the nearby country of Malawi, which borders Tanzania, Zambia, and Zimbabwe. It reminded me that in life, there are no meaningless details. Upon arriving in Malawi, we stopped at a phone store to purchase SIM cards for our mobile devices. As we waited for the transaction to be completed, I noticed on the wall a huge quote by Nelson Mandela. It reminded me of not only his commitment to living the beyond ordinary life, but also his impact around the world.

It read: "*What counts in life is not the mere fact that we have lived; it is what difference we have made to the lives of others that will determine the significance of the life we leave.*"

Certainly, Mandela's life and legacy were marked not only by vision and tenacity, but also excellence. Mandela was tempted to live a life of "average," a life of good, but he knew that goodness wasn't good enough.

It was greatness and the desire for excellence in all areas of his life that motivated him to live a life of significance.

In Mandela's life and in ours, we might ask ourselves: "What does excellence look like? How do I move beyond good and live a life of great?"

Over the years I have had the honor of being a part of a nonprofit charity that has offered help and hope to tens of thousands of children and families. When you are trying your very best to offer help to people, many times you succeed; sometimes you don't. Many times, efforts to assist people have fallen short. Good hearts and good intentions don't always yield good results. I've learned from our mistakes. We've applied best practices in a spirit of excellence to make sure we can better help more people. At times, I'm reminded of our failures; it helps me make sure I stay on track to do good, be Great.

Good Wasn't Good Enough for David

The first time I saw David was while he was faithfully volunteering every day at our community center. It was unusual to see someone volunteer all day every day, so after about a month, I asked one of our staff members to ask him a few questions and find out what his story was. I wasn't prepared for the answer I was about to receive.

"Pastor Scott, David sleeps under our food truck every night," the staff member told me. "He's been sleeping on our campus for months. He spends night after night living under our truck."

I couldn't believe it. It took me a few days to fully process the story. David was a war veteran—no family, few friends, and dealing with stage 3 cancer. It began to make sense to me why he was on our campus every day without fail, willing to do whatever we asked of him. He had nowhere else to go.

David had a wonderful personality and work ethic, in spite of his situation. He was a joy to work with, and it was rewarding watching him serve others.

I remember telling our staff that no one on my watch was going to live under our truck. I was determined to find out how we could somehow help him out of his situation. I made a few phone calls and arranged for David to stay in a nearby motor home park. I happened to know the owner of the property, and after a phone call and discussion, he agreed to knock down the cost a bit. We made arrangements and finalized the opportunity for David to move. We collected furniture and all the fixtures from our thrift center and filled the place with everything he would need to begin over and live a dignified life. Food was not a challenge, since we operated a very large food bank on property. He was all set. Everything would be great, I thought. We all would feel good about helping David out.

For about thirty days, it worked out well. Every day we would see David, and he was energetic and appreciative. He knew the rules laid out for him, and for the first few weeks, he did well. But after about the second month, calls started coming in from nearby residents and the property manager complaining about David. It wasn't until I visited him and went inside that I realized we had a real problem.

The place was an absolute wreck in every regard. food, trash, and clothes were everywhere; it was the worst I had ever seen. It didn't take me long to figure out that we had done David a disservice by our "good works." In reality, good wasn't good for David, or for us. The donors weren't happy, the staff felt disregarded, and David knew he had failed. Everyone lost. In our haste to do good, we didn't use best practices and did more harm than good.

We should have done much more in the way of comprehensive counseling and support services. We had moved David too quickly, and he wasn't mentally or socially prepared for the move. It was a culture shock for him. No one was more shocked than we were, however. If I had only known then what I know now, I would not have intervened the way I had. I would have moved slower and more thoroughly. I would have done a better job at doing good. We failed David and we failed ourselves, but it was a valuable lesson that helped us move from simply doing good to do good, be Great, in a spirit of excellence.

Great Lessons We Can Learn from Shark Tank on Do Good, Be Great

I love watching *Shark Tank*. It's one of my favorite TV shows. For those of you unfamiliar with it, product inventors and business entrepreneurs—wannabe millionaires—have a few minutes to make their pitch in front of million-aires and billionaire business celebrities/investors. The show is brutal. Gut-wrenching honesty and dog-eat-dog personalities create an atmosphere for drama, competition, and negotiations for potentially, the next big product or business to hit the streets. You have the bait, which happens to be the inventor and his idea, and then you have the sharks, hungry for another meal with blood in the water—all in a thirty-minute window.

I guess what I like the most about the show is that in most cases, it is the perfect case of taking a good product and making it great. In seconds, these brilliant sharks take a good idea— and you can see the wheels spinning in their heads as they do this—and with a little tweaking and adjusting, suddenly come up with a way to make the good, Great. In an instant, an average idea becomes extraordinary and a small-time inventor "suddenly" becomes a huge success. Through the process of evaluation, critical thinking and gut level honesty, a good idea becomes a hit.

Much like the small-time inventor or entrepreneur, we need to take a few of our approaches and ways of doing things and throw them in the shark tank so we can move from good to great, or do good, be Great.

Goodness Isn't Good Enough

I first heard this phrase from a nonprofit expert whose job it was to evaluate nonprofits and report back to leaders interested in investing in their community through philanthropic giving. When I first heard him say the phrase "goodness isn't good enough," it so resonated within me that I had to go back to my office and write the phrase down so I wouldn't miss out on this powerful and impacting thought.

Many of us, I believe, still believe that goodness is enough. I believe that there are generations that live by the motto that we all do a little good and leave the results where they may. Currently in the United States, there are 47 million people living in poverty. That's an awful lot of people struggling in poverty, many of them in generational poverty unable to move forward. At the same time, there are more nonprofits and charities than ever before in the US, according to Forbes December 2014 report.

What Would the Sharks Say?

- What you are doing isn't working.
- Your efforts are admirable, but we're lacking results.
- You're spinning your wheels, but you're not going anywhere.
- Stop the madness.

This principle certainly applies to every area of our lives. It's not limited to the nonprofit or church world. Whether in your personal life or finances or relationships, it's healthy and necessary to stop and evaluate to see if it's possible to move from good to great.

What Does Excellence Look Like?

I get a lot of joy from hearing my friends and neighbors say that my children look and act like me. Many times my friends will say, "Man . . . Aaren looks just like you," or "Austen is a chip off the ol' block," or "Amanda is so much like you," or "Allison is your twin." I love hearing that my children look and act like the old man. So when someone asks, "What does Scott look like?" you might hear it said, "If you've seen his children, then you know what Scott looks and acts like." So it is with greatness.

What does greatness look like? Just as our children look like us and resemble us, there are characteristics in our lives that are very similar when we look at excellence.

There is a story in the Bible about a young man named Daniel. The king at that time was looking for a few good leaders. He assembled a group of young, potential leaders so he could see if any of them had all the qualities and attributes necessary to lead and stand above the crowd.

The story goes on to say that when the king took note of Daniel, he surmised that Daniel had a "spirit of excellence." I love that phrase, "a spirit of excellence." I'm not really sure that if we had the opportunity to ask the king what a spirit of excellence looks like that he would know. I think the king may have had a hard time articulating exactly what he meant by that or what specific characteristics he saw.

I think Daniel had what I mentioned in previous chapters: the "it factor." This spirit of excellence was noticeable and tangible; it wasn't limited to his outward characteristics alone. I think the king could see qualities and attributes that were unseen to the naked eye, but very noticeable to him. I believe Daniel possessed something far greater than good looks, charisma, and personality. Daniel was great, both outwardly and inwardly, and that made for the right ingredients for something very, very special.

What Excellence Looks Like

Let's explore what excellence may look like. Hopefully we will discern that some characteristics and traits that were evident in Daniel and Nelson Mandela are in you, too.

1. Excellence starts from the inside out.

Israeli businesswoman and philanthropist Shari Arison said it best: *"Doing good holds the power to transferring us on the inside, and then ripple out in ever-exploding circles that positively impact the world at large."* [11] Excellence begins on the inside and then works itself outside to touch the people around you, and your community and world.

2. Excellence watches its relationships carefully.

Think of the five people closest to you, that you spend the most time with, or that you go to lunch with or hang out with on the weekend. Write down their names and put a number next to each one (1=lowest/negative, 10=highest/positive). Think about their reputation, skill sets, character, integrity, values, and so on. Total the score of all five friends and divide by five to see the average score. If you score a total from ten to twenty, know you have some work to do. If your range is twenty-five to thirty-five, you are surrounded with average friends. If your score is in the forty to fifty range, you have made the right choice of surrounding yourself with people of excellence.

Please remember that it's not too late to choose great friends and colleagues. You will be very glad you surrounded yourself with people of excellence who will inspire you, motivate you, challenge you, and hopefully, change you.

3. Excellence develops the courage to take risks.

Those who have a spirit of excellence are not afraid of change and have developed the confidence to take risks. Excellent leaders have learned that leadership requires action, not just theory. I love the poem from the Brick Quantum Leap thinking, called *"Risking"*:

To laugh is to risk appearing the fool.
To weep is to risk appearing sentimental.
To reach out for another is to risk involvement.
To expose your feelings is to risk exposing your true self.
To place your ideas and your dreams before a crowd is to risk embarrassment.
To love is to risk not being loved in return.
To live is to risk dying.
To hope is to risk despair.
To try is to risk failure.
But risks must be taken, because the greatest hazard in life is to risk nothing at all.
The person who risks nothing does nothing, has nothing, and is nothing.
They may avoid suffering and sorrow, but they cannot learn, feel, change, grow, love, or live.
Chained by their certitudes, they are slaves. They have forfeited their freedom.
Only a person who risks is free. [12]
(Love Unlimited)

I love what Katherine Mansfield, the famous British short-story writer once said:

Risk! Risk anything! Care no more for the opinion of others, for those voices.
Do the hardest thing on earth for you. Act for yourself. Face the truth.
(Katherine Mansfield, British short-story writer)

4. *Excellence looks for and discovers new opportunities.*
People with a spirit of excellence live and walk with an eye for what I call, "divine opportunities." They have an eye to see windows of opportunity that most people never see or are unaware exist. The word "opportunity" has an interesting meaning. In the Greek, it is *kairos*, an ancient Greek word meaning, "the right or opportune moment (the supreme moment)."[13]

It is a term from a Bible verse about making the most of every opportunity: *"making the most of every opportunity, because the days are evil"* (Ephesians 5:16, NIV). "Opportunity" is a layman's term used by ship captains in the old days. The captains would look for the right season and time—the exact moment—to order their crews to bring their ships into port. They wouldn't just randomly turn the ship into port without carefully observing the wind, tides, currents, seas, and so on. When everything lined up just right, they would view it as the "right opportunity" and head for the port.

People of excellence have learned the skill of recognizing the right time. And when they see it, they seize it.

I like what Pat Williams, senior vice president of the NBA's Orlando Magic, says in his book *Coach Wooden's Greatest Secret* about excellence:

1. You are in school for an education. Keep that first in your thoughts; play basketball second.
2. Do not cut classes and do be on time.
3. Do not fall behind and do get your work in on time.
4. Have regular study hours and keep them.
5. Arrange with your professors in advance when you must be absent.
6. Do not expect favors. Do your part.
7. Arrange for tutoring at the first sign of trouble.
8. Work for a high grade point average. Do not be satisfied by merely meeting the eligibility requirements.
9. Do your assignments to the best of your ability, but never be too proud to seek help and advice.
10. Earn the respect of everyone.[14]

5. Excellence boldly goes the second mile.

If you desire to live a life of excellence and live the beyond ordinary life, one of the keys to living it is a willingness to go the extra mile. I call them "second-milers." Jesus once said, *"If anyone forces you to go one mile, go with them two miles"* (Matthew 5:41, NIV). Most people are content to go only the distance that is required. Just give them the minimum requirement, and that's exactly what they will do; nothing more, nothing less.

Excellence teaches us to be willing to go above and beyond—to go two miles when only one is required. Our society has trained us to do only what is expected, but those who want to do good, and be Great have an innate ability of going far beyond average. They go the second mile. I can't help but think about the benefit and blessing you receive by living with this attitude of excellence.

6. Excellence gives up to go up.

A person who has a spirit of excellence has learned the principle of "giving up." Nothing is truly achieved by hanging on. You get to go up when you learn to give up. You limit how high you go by what you hang onto. People who live beyond ordinary lives have mastered this principle and live by it daily. Nothing is accomplished without sacrifice.

As I'm writing this book, I have to let go of some things in order to have the time to write—it may be leisure activities, TV, or a hobby. Those who desire to have a spirit of excellence understand that dedication and sacrifice help pave the way for you to go up. I remember my son Aaren demonstrated this principle for me one day when he was a small boy. This boy loved to eat with both hands full—and his mouth full, too. So there he was one day, sitting in his high chair with two cookies, one in each hand. I got a bigger, better, and absolutely mouthwatering cookie. He looked at his cookie in his left hand first, but then looked in his right hand. Then he looked at the cookie I was dangling before him. After several long seconds, the principle of "give up and go up" hit him. In our little kitchen, he received a revelation some adults have never discovered: He had to let go of what he was holding onto in order to embrace what was in front of him. As a very young boy, he realized he couldn't have it all. He learned that he had to let go in order to grab what his eye was focused on. When he discovered this lesson, he was so glad he did! He was so very happy he let go so that he had the capacity to get the new cookie. I enjoyed watching my boy live out this principle.

You will be just as happy, if not more, by learning from this cute story a powerful truth that can liberate you and give you a new future. Aaren had to let go of a cookie; as adults, we need to let go of things that are far weightier and more practical.

Excellence is needed more than ever when one is dealing with hurting and wounded people who are desperate and feel abandoned. What better way to demonstrate one's compassion and care than to express it helping others?

Our campus in downtown Orlando helps more than 500 people a day. Although many times we fail, our goal is to provide first-class service with a heart filled with compassion and a spirit of excellence. On a monthly basis, our leadership teams focus on making sure our staff, board, and volunteers are helping people with excellence and compassion. Each day I'm reminded how critical it is for all of us to have our "game face" on, because so many people are depending on us to treat them with dignity and respect.

People like Barbara need us to walk in a spirit of excellence. Her story challenges me on daily to do good, be Great with excellence.

I Hope What Happened to Me Doesn't Happen to You

It was just another day when I had the privilege of taking a group of guests on tour of our campus ministry. On tours, you never really know what's going to happen. Each one is full of adventure. Every day, more than 500 people in need fill our campus. The parking lot is full; the crisis center, medical clinic, and food bank are always full of wonderful people who come to us weekly for help, counseling, and encouragement.

Little did I know that on our lunch tour that day, we would have an encounter that would shape us and challenge us. Our encounter was with Barbara, a middle-aged woman who lived in the MetroWest area of Orlando, just a few miles west of our campus. Years before, when I first met Barbara, she was living a pretty good life. She was married, lived in the suburbs, had a good job, enjoyed healthy relationships, and had a bright future ahead of her. She was even one of our donors. She never would have dreamed that she would be a client in our crisis center just a few years later. In fact, she was one of a number of donors who became our clients during the Great Recession of 2009. Much to her dismay, she had to ask for help from the very ones she had assisted financially through monthly donations.

The lunch tour was going great, but then it got even better. A small group of twenty business leaders were circled up in our crisis center listening to my talk about our programs, when suddenly, Barbara burst into the circle and pointed her finger at each one of my lunch guests while staring intensely into their eyes. Even the strongest people in the group straightened up and took notice. "I hope what happened to me doesn't happen to you!" Barbara said to them, eyeing each one. She took her time turning to each one, making sure she had their full attention. The eyes of everyone on the tour enlarged by at least 200 percent, and a few jaws dropped open as well. Even I was caught a bit off guard for the first few seconds; but after that I knew this would be good for Barbara and great for us on the tour.

After gaining everyone's attention, she proceeded to tell the group her dilemma. She had a good job, great marriage, and bright future until one day when she was in a traffic accident. She was hit from behind, and as a result, her life unraveled so quickly that, in a matter of months, she would lose her health, her marriage, her job, her house, her dignity . . . and her hope.

One accident that was not her fault had thrown her into a tailspin from which it would take her years to fully recover. She proceeded to tell the group that she was at the campus for assistance, encouragement, and help.

She gave a passionate description of the help she was receiving from our staff and the programs we offered. I couldn't have scripted it any better. She concluded her two-minute speech by repeating the ten words that still ring in my heart after all these years, and hopefully still ring in the hearts of each one who attended the tour that day: "I hope what happened to me doesn't happen to you!"

Although I didn't plan on this "divine encounter" with Barbara and my guests on the tour that day, I was so very glad our paths met. (I was also glad that Barbara didn't share a complaint or gripe, had there been one!) What I heard Barbara say was that she was grateful, full of hope, and had not been treated like a number, statistic, or faceless person. I heard Barbara say that we had treated her with dignity and a spirit of excellence.

Barbara understood opposition. For the first time in her life, she had been confronted with medical issues, relationship problems, and financial circumstances that cripple many. She responded with faith, tenacity, and determination to overcome her struggles and lived for seeing each new day filled with purpose, destiny, and hope. I saw Barbara a few years later, and thankfully, she had recovered, although the hurt and pain from her opposition—poverty—was still real and raw.

When I am faced with struggles and trials, I think of people like Barbara who display such courage and character in tough times—people who could easily throw in the towel and say, "I quit!" but they don't. They keep fighting despite the obstacles they face. It's people like Barbara who inspire me to keep fighting. I take away valuable lessons from people like her. They motivate me to keep going in spite of the battles I face. Barbara did well in the face of opposition. Whether you are facing the enemies of poverty, sickness, divorce, discouragement, and more; how you respond will determine your destiny.

The culture of excellence is contagious. From our board members to our volunteers, you can see and feel that each person is valuable. Each person is not defined by his or her circumstances. Each person has a bright future.

Questions for you on ....
Chapter 4: When Goodness Isn't Good Enough

1. When you read about Nelson Mandela, what are some of the do good be great qualities you see?

2. Pick out one of the quotes from Nelson Mandela and discuss why this particular quote inspires you.

3. What would the sharks say about your life if you had to make a presentation to them about your life, leadership skills and lifestyle in general?

4. What does excellence look like to you? List a time recently where you went beyond average to live a life of excellence?

5. If you have to give up to go up, what areas do you need to give up to go to the next level of excellence?

6. If excellence is going the second mile, in what areas of your life have you stopped at mile one and need to change and begin to go the second mile?

Notes

Great Quotes from a Great Leader
Oprah Winfrey

- *"The more you praise and celebrate your life, the more there is in life to celebrate."*
- *"Real integrity is doing the right thing, knowing that nobody's going to know whether you did it or not."*
- *"My philosophy is that not only are you responsible for your life, but doing the best at this moment puts you in the best place for the next moment."*
- *"If you want your life to be more rewarding, you have to change the way you think."*
- *"Every one of us gets through the tough times because somebody is there, standing in the gap to close it for us."*
- *"Let your light shine. Shine within you so that it can shine on someone else. Let your light shine."*
- *"In order to be truly happy, you must live along with, and you must stand for something larger than yourself."*
- *"If you're hurting, you need to help somebody else ease their hurt. If you're in pain, help somebody else's pain."*
- *"My constant prayer for myself is to be used in service for the greater good."*
- *"When you're doing the work you're meant to do, it feels right and every day is a bonus, regardless of what you're getting paid."*
- *"You really haven't changed, you've just become more of yourself. That is really what we're all trying to do: become more of ourselves."*

5

Do Good, Be Great by Harnessing the Power of Habit

KEY 5: BEYOND
ORDINARY PEOPLE PRACTICE THE POWER OF HABIT

OPRAH WINFREY—Do Good, Be Great for Those without Purpose

As a highly influential talk show host, philanthropist, author, and actress, Oprah Winfrey has played a key role in modern American life. She has shaped cultural trends, promoted causes, and through her television talk shows and books, has addressed many of the social issues women face. In particular, she has been an important role model for black women, helping by way of her own achievements to break down social and cultural barriers to success.

The Bible contains the exhortation: *"Who dares despise the day of small things..."* (Zechariah 4:10, NIV). Certainly Oprah demonstrates that a small or humble beginning does not have to set boundaries on do good, be Great. She is an example to all of us that personal circumstances and upbringing can neither stop a legacy of do good, be Great, nor limit how far and wide its influence will stretch.

Oprah was born January 29, 1954, on a farm in Kosciusko, Mississippi, to unmarried parents who broke up soon after her conception. After their separation, Oprah was left in the care of her maternal grandmother, on the farm.

She had a difficult childhood. She lived in great poverty as a youngster and often wore potato sacks as her school dresses, for which she was belittled. Starting at age nine, she became a victim of serial sexual abuse that did not stop until she was a teenager. She was named for the biblical Orpah (see Ruth 1:4), but due to difficulty of spelling and ease of pronunciation, she was called "Oprah" nearly from birth.

Even as a child, her destiny in entertainment tugged at her interests, as she found great pleasure in playacting before an audience of farm animals. Not shy in public, she addressed her church congregation about "when Jesus rose on Easter Day" when she was only two years old. Under her grandmother's strict guidance, she learned to read at age two-and-a-half. As she grew up, she was shuttled between her mother in Milwaukee, Wisconsin, and her father in Nashville, Tennessee, until finally settling down with her father at age fourteen.

Oprah has said that her father "saved her life" by providing strict guidance, structure, and rules in the home. His life of discipline taught her that practicing healthy habits was foundational to living a successful life. Many years later, the power of habit she had learned as a young teen became a core value in her talk shows and books, where she stressed the relation of good habits to succeeding at self-improvement and self-help.

With her father's tutoring, Oprah became an excellent student. When her speech-making prowess once earned her $500, she decided she wanted to be "paid to talk." When she was nineteen and still a sophomore in college, she became Nashville's first African-American female co-anchor of the evening television news.

Oprah moved to Chicago, Illinois, in January 1984 to further her television career, and in 1985 created the one hour *Oprah Winfrey Show*. That year, musician Quincy Jones saw her on television and cast her for Steven Spielberg's *The Color Purple*, and her popularity skyrocketed.

Having already harnessed the power of habit as a young woman, Oprah began to implement it with passion as an adult. Using her newfound fame as a platform, she launched a lifetime lifelong ambition of do good, be Great, by both helping and inspiring others to better their lives:

- **1987**—Her own private charity, The Oprah Winfrey Foundation, was established to support women, children, and families throughout the world.
- **1991**—Oprah testified before the US Senate Judiciary Committee, seeking to establish a national database of convicted child abusers.
- **1993**—President Clinton, taking action as a result of her testimony, signed into law the National Child Protection Act.
- **1994**—Oprah launched the Family for Better Lives Foundation; an experiment in shifting people from welfare to work that eventually did not succeed.
- **1996**—Declaring she wanted "to get the country reading," Oprah announced she was starting an on-air reading club. The club's popularity exploded, and within a year she was the most powerful book marketer in America.
- **1997**— Oprah created the Angel Network, a public charity with a stated mission to "inspire people and make a difference in the lives of others." The nonprofit would provide grants to charities involved in combating poverty, homelessness, child neglect, and disease. Her network raised more than $51 million for charitable programs.
- **1999**—Oxygen Media debuted, a company Oprah co-founded to produce cable and Internet programming for women.
- **2002**—The inaugural Bob Hope Humanitarian Award was given to Oprah in recognition of her pioneer status in the entertainment industry and her humanitarian efforts.
- **2005**—A dedicated activist for children's rights, Oprah launched Oprah's Child Predator Watch List and pledged a $100,000 reward per case to anyone the FBI or local law officials said provided information leading to the capture and arrest of fugitives featured on *The Oprah Winfrey Show* or Oprah.com. Since its launch, nine of the featured fugitives have been captured.
- **2011**—*The Oprah Winfrey Show*, now syndicated, was seen on more than 200 US stations and in more than one hundred countries. Oprah launched the Oprah Winfrey Network (OWN) cable channel.

- **2013**—President Obama awarded Oprah the Presidential Medal of Freedom, the nation's highest civilian honor, for her contributions to the betterment of the country.

According to *Forbes*, Oprah was the wealthiest African-American of the twentieth century and the world's only black billionaire for three consecutive years. *Business Week* named her the greatest black philanthropist in American history. Yet Oprah was neither born into privilege nor had a family heritage of wealth and status that gave her an edge in life. She did not despise her "small beginning" by letting the sexual abuse and poverty stop her. As a result, she today models the fact that following after good daily choices, decisions, and habits can lead you to do a world of good, Great.

"I don't think of myself as a poor, deprived ghetto girl who made good," Oprah says. "I think of myself as somebody who from an early age knew I was responsible for myself, and I had to make good. You cannot blame your parents, your circumstances—because you are not your circumstances. You are your possibilities. If you know that, you can do anything." We make our habits and then our habits turn around and make us.

It's very obvious that Oprah Winfrey has disciplined herself and found the key to healthy habits that have helped her over the years to accomplish so much for so many people all over the world. Her life of do good, be Great should serve as a model for us all as we aspire to live beyond ordinary lives. Coach Wooden, much like Oprah, learned at an early age the power of healthy habits. Pat Williams, in his book, *Coach Wooden's Greatest Secrets*, reveals key habits that Coach Wooden not only lived by, but also motivated his players and coaches to embrace and live by.

Beyond Ordinary Habits
Start Building Healthy Habits

1. Build a habit of focusing on one habit at a time.
2. Build a habit of focusing on adding good habits, not breaking bad habits.

3. Build a habit of awakening early.
4. Build a habit of starting each day with positive thoughts.
5. Build a habit of daily exercise.
6. Build a habit of thankfulness
7. Build a habit of learning something new every day.
8. Build a habit of smiling at people.
9. Build a habit of giving people sincere, heartfelt compliments.
10. Build a habit of saying, "I love you."
11. Build a habit of truly listening to other people.
12. Build a habit of carefully considering requests for your time before you say yes.
13. Build a habit of saving money.
14. Build a habit of spending significant time with your family.
15. Build a habit of tidying up every day. Clean up the clutter.
16. Build a daily habit of writing out a to-do list.
17. Build a habit to review each day before you go to bed.
18. Build a habit of hitting the sack at a reasonable time.[14]

A Place Where Hope Happens

In this chapter, I'm going to introduce you to some friends of mine. Some, I've known for many years, others for only a few. You'll meet Joel Hunter, Regina Hill, Leo Jones, and John Morgan.

One is a nationally known Central Florida pastor. One is an Orlando City Commissioner. One is a wonderful man who has struggled to care for his ailing wife, and who rides a bike around town looking for work so he can get help for his wife. One is Central Florida's most visible and prominent attorney. These four people are all very different, and from different walks of life. All are from different parts of town. All have different occupations, different friends, and different philosophies. However, they all have one thing in common: Each has been impacted and touched by the mission of the Community Food and Outreach Center.

They all, in one way or another, give generously *to* the mission, or they have been given much *by* the ministry. For all of them, their lives have all intersected at 150 West Michigan Street, in downtown Orlando; a place "where hope happens."

Habit #1: Touch Others with a Touch of Destiny
Joel Hunter, Northland: A Church Distributed – Distributing Hope

I must admit that Thanksgiving is the third best day of the year for me (the first best being my wedding anniversary on July 26th, and the second best, my birthday on October 30th). I love the fact that on Thanksgiving, I can sit with my family and enjoy a wonderful time of gratitude, while in the back of my mind, realize that thousands of people are enjoying a similar kind of meal and time with family and loved ones.

Thanksgiving is also always a very busy time of year for the Community Food and Outreach Center. It was especially busy and meaningful in 2014 because of two very special people I interacted with over that November holiday season: Joel Hunter and Leo Jones. Little did I know that Joel and Leo—two people who didn't know each other—would come together in my life to make Thanksgiving 2014 a holiday I would never forget.

It began with Joel Hunter, the senior pastor of Northland: A Church Distributed, in Longwood, Florida, near Orlando. Joel is a man with a heart of gold, and by far one of the most influential leaders in our community, state, and nation. He is a quality leader with an incredible heart for others—especially the poor and needy. A few months ago, Joel and I spoke at the Conference on Poverty and Compassion, I reminded him of the story that follows.

I was considering and faithfully praying about starting the charity in Orlando now called Community Food and Outreach Center. It must have been back in the late 1990s, and I was unsure if this was something I should do. I had met with several dozen families, friends, and respected leaders to get their advice and insight, and Joel happened to be on my list of people whose insight and opinion I wanted. I was struggling with either pastoring a local church in Orlando or doing the charity work full time. After pouring my heart out to Joel for more than thirty minutes, he patiently waited, and then with great wisdom and insight simply said: "Scott, there are 2,000 churches in Central Florida. We don't need another church; we need a community center to help the poor."

Looking back over all the years and the hundreds of thousands of families that have been helped, I am so very glad I listened to Joel, followed my heart, and listened to his guidance.

Just a few months later, I got a call from Joel's office and one of his assistants left a message that there was a check waiting for me to pick up at their church office. The message also said that the church had collected a Thanksgiving offering and wanted to help our ministry out. I really hate to admit this, but over the years I've learned that most times, when a church says they have a check for you, it's usually for less than a hundred dollars. Although I didn't think this was the case with Northland, my first reaction was not to drop everything and head on over. I thought, *I'm sure this can wait a few days*, so off I went into the activity of organizing all the details of the upcoming food drive and distribution.

Now back to Thanksgiving 2014. During that Thanksgiving holiday, we partnered with over thirty public and private schools in the Orlando area for a Thanksgiving food drive called Neighbors Helping Neighbors. Schools were getting ready and volunteers were mobilizing and getting excited about this great event. Our partners were interviewing families and putting all the details in place.

I was so consumed with the event I completely forgot about Joel and Northland's phone message until I received a second call and message reminding me of the check. It was the last sentence of the assistant's message that finally got my attention and caused me to drop everything and head over to Longwood, ASAP. "I really think you will be excited to see this check," she said. "If I were you, I'd come as soon as I could." That's when I made my way over and picked up the Thanksgiving offering.

It was a bit awkward after I received the check. I certainly didn't want to open it right there in the office, so I placed it in my coat pocket and thanked them a few dozen times. I didn't want to open the check in the parking lot either, so I waited until I was in my car and driving south on State Road 17-92. I finally got up the nerve to open the envelope and see what was inside. I felt for a moment like I was at the Grammys or the Oscars, waiting for the big moment. In hindsight, I should have pulled over on the side of the road because that's exactly where I ended up after I opened the envelope: Northland Church had given us $35,000!

My heart was filled with joy and gratitude. I thought of all the wonderful members of that church, and the leaders and pastors. Their good-hearted people had given so graciously and generously. My mind immediately raced to all the families that would be blessed a few days later, on Thanksgiving. That offering also ensures that we could do even more than we had planned.

Habit #2: Touch Others with a Touch of Hope
I can't leave here without telling someone
Each year, we focus a few weeks on reaching out to our state and local politicians. Usually in September we organize lunches called "poverty summits," and invite other nonprofit leaders to educate our local and state leaders on poverty and specific issues related to poverty, such as homelessness, domestic violence, and medical care for the poor. One luncheon was particularly special, though at the time I had no idea of the impact it would have on me. When it was over, it emphasized again the importance of our method of helping families out of poverty by offering them a *hand up*, not a *handout*. About halfway through a tour of our 50,000 square-foot ministry center I was conducting for about twenty politicians—right in the middle of the speech I was giving, and out of the blue—one of the politicians said with conviction and emotion, "I can't leave here without telling somebody!"

I remember right where I was standing the moment she said it; I was at the top of the loading ramp overlooking our food center, and the unexpected interruption had such an impact on me that I almost fell over the railing. It took everyone a few seconds to figure out what was going on. And of course, being the hospitable tour guide, I stopped my presentation and let her have the floor. No one on the tour of about twenty politicians had any idea what she was about to say or the impact her words would have on validating our programs and our model for helping the working poor of our community.

"Pastor George," she said, "you don't know this—in fact, I have never told anybody what I'm about to say. For the last four years, I came to your campus every week for help and a little hope. I am a nurse, I had a job—a good job—but I just couldn't make it and I needed a little help. As a single mom, I was taking care of my child, my disabled brother, and my father who was well along in years and needed my care. I was able to pay my mortgage each month. And though it was tight, I could pay my car payment as well. But it seemed like I could never get to the place where I could pay for the food to feed my growing family of four on my income alone. It was hard, but one day I heard about this place. When I came I was amazed at the program that was in place to give me a hand during a very difficult time in my life."

However, what she said next left everyone speechless. "Many of you now know me as the new City of Orlando Commissioner Regina Hill, but a few years ago, I was just a single mom struggling to get by. I'm so very grateful that this place was open and your people welcomed me with open arms and open hearts to give me a chance to get help in a dignified way."

The shock took a few seconds to settle in. Here we were listening to an Orlando city commissioner who, a few years before her election to one of the most powerful positions in our city, was a client and recipient of our services. It just so happens that most of the people we serve week after week live in the district Regina now oversees. More families come from her district than any other area of our city.

I was blown away. I had no idea of her history. I don't remember much from the rest of the tour and luncheon because I was so overwhelmed and grateful that we were able to come alongside her and her family and offer a bit of help.

Habit #3: Touch Others with a Touch of Compassion
Leo: A Story of Desperation and Determination

In the fall of 2008, we had just completed our Thanksgiving fund campaign. After months of preparation, we had finally finished and were getting ready to enjoy this holiday with our families.

Needless to say, the Thanksgiving event was flawless and executed with excellence. All the food had been delivered and distributed, and it came time to rest and spend time with my family. As always, the best part of the day was seeing all my family members and offering a prayer of thanksgiving. Though I am one of several pastors in the family, I usually say the prayer; but that year was different. I asked each person to say a few words and then we'd let the prayer build on what the person before them prayed. All I had to do was say "amen" at the end.

Since I wasn't praying, all I could think about was all the people in our community who would be having a healthy meal thanks to our donors, volunteers, and staff. Sometimes I feel a bit frustrated because though I do a lot of work, I often do not see the end results. However, this year would be different. It would be a Thanksgiving I would never forget.

After the meal, we all took part in the usual Thanksgiving ritual; we moaned and groaned and all went to lie down and watch the Green Bay Packers play the Detroit Lions. The living room floor was full. As usual, the ladies had not eaten as much as the guys, so several of them simply made their way to the dining room table for a card game, while a few others made their way into the kitchen to tackle the dishes and cleanup duties.

All of a sudden, there was a knock at our front door. Since it was my house and I was the only one of the men and boys who could move, I got up and answered the door. Little did I know, the next few moments would help shape me and my heart to continue to do good.

I opened the door and there was an old, African-American man standing on the step with a hose and bucket in his hand. I see people every day who are struggling and hurting in downtown Orlando, but very seldom do I encounter the poor and needy in my suburban neighborhood. I had seen the man before, riding around the community on his bike with a bucket and hose, and I often wondered what he was doing. That day I would find out.

He was polite and humble, yet seemed tired—exhausted even. He started the conversation by saying he did not want me to give him any money. He wanted to work for any money I could give him. I knew immediately he was legitimate and knew he was telling the truth, but I wanted to find out more. I was ready to give him some money, but I felt like I needed to listen and hear what was going on. It would have been easy to simply give him some money to get him on his way, but I felt this would be a valuable lesson for both of us. So I asked him a few questions and suddenly the floodgates opened.

His name was Leo Jones. He was taking care of his sick wife. She had a terminal illness and he would ride his bike throughout Central Florida looking for odd jobs so he could afford medical expenses, diapers for her, and food for them both. He was insistent that he would work for any money that I was willing to give him. Knowing this was an unusual encounter for both of us, I immediately invited him into my house and offered to fix him a traditional George family Thanksgiving dinner. As far as I was concerned, he had been sent by God to my house that day and he was part of our family.

By now, all the guys were snoring and asleep on the living room floor, the ladies were having fun and laughing. Though they seemed excited to meet our new friend, Leo, they were not sure what to do. It was a bit odd, but not uncomfortable. I knew what was going on; this was my encounter to feel the pain, see a face, and hear firsthand on Thanksgiving Day one story of the people in my community. Leo represented thousands of people in Central Florida for me; he was the voice and face of those I was committed to serve.

We sat outside on the porch for more than two hours. I was glued to his every word. We laughed and we cried. He told me some incredible stories about his photography business, his love for music, and how he would travel around the state of Florida with his band, playing gospel music until his wife became sick. Once that happened, he lost his business and could no longer travel to inspire others with his songs. I then did what my mom always did. "Eat some more food . . . Get some more turkey, gravy, and apple pie," I insisted.

Thankfully, I remembered to pack him a few plates to take home to his precious wife. I would not let him work on Thanksgiving. I went around and took a few bucks from the guys who were sleeping to make sure that he wouldn't have to work for the next few days (and could hopefully spend some time with his wife instead). I invited him to our campus in downtown to meet with one of our social workers to see how we could help long-term. It sounds like I tried to help him that day, but he helped me out so much more. I fed him turkey—he fed me passion. I gave him apple pie—he gave me purpose. I got to see and hear the stories of the people I loved serving.

A divine encounter like that had never happened before. It was a wonderful reminder to me to keep my priorities in the right spot; to stay passionate and energetic about helping the poor, and to keep my love strong for the underdog. Leo changed my life and kept my heart soft for those who needed a hand up during difficult times. It was the best Thanksgiving ever thanks to Joel and Leo, two men who had never met, but who both taught me valuable life lessons on giving and receiving.

Habit #4: Touch Others with a Touch of Generosity
John and Curtis: A Clinic for the People
It was 5,000 square feet of raw, empty warehouse space. It didn't look like much. Those with expert eyes would likely look at it and shake their heads in disgust. I looked at it and was gripped by a sense of promise and destiny. Week after week, I would walk past the space and say aloud, "This is our clinic." I'm glad no one else was around because they would have thought I was crazy.

In the beginning, I felt a bit crazy. One day, I asked my trusted right-hand/executive director to come with me to the warehouse to dream and speak life where the clinic would be. We both felt funny doing this, but after we did it, we noticed the momentum and atmosphere started to change. It felt good.

After a few weeks of this, we met with one of our key board members, and with a little faith (and a bit of trepidation), shared the vision for the clinic. We hoped we wouldn't get laughed out of the building. To our amazement, the board member caught on and started believing with us, even joining us in speaking the vision: "This is our clinic."

After a few more weeks, we met with the entire board and staff, and suddenly, any hint of fear was gone. A spirit of faith filled the entire warehouse space as we all spoke words of life and purpose. Nothing had changed—naturally speaking—but something unseen was happening. It didn't take long before we all knew the clinic was going to happen. Every day we would simply speak what we believed. Boy, was it fun to watch and see the power of our words bring life to that space. It is remarkable what can happen when people start speaking life, purpose, and destiny.

The Clinic For the People

Many experts told us it couldn't be done, but we fought through the opposition and continued on our path as time rolled on. Finally, in 2006, we connected with a few volunteer nurses and doctors, and started to open our campus to offer medical help on Sunday mornings—the only morning our facility wasn't packed with people. It felt strange for me to miss Sunday morning church services, but I was reminded that what we were doing was "church outpoured," and by serving moms, dads, children, and senior citizens each Sunday, I was in the right place doing the right thing. We were up and running, though our clinic was raw and simple—they were humble beginnings. At first we set up a sign-in table and six examination rooms within the center. Each was equipped with a six-foot-long white, plastic folding table, which we covered with white clinical paper, and a few sheets hung around each one for privacy. With volunteers set to maintain the records, greeters to meet those who needed medical attention, and a few nurses and doctors, we were on our way.

The first few months, our clinic was a bit sketchy, but our love and care were genuine. What we lacked in professionalism we made up for with passion. We treated every person who came in with dignity and respect and offered them first-class service.

The patients didn't care about the décor. They were grateful and appreciative to have access to medical care, as they had no other options. After a few months, people flocked to the clinic. Each Sunday, we served hundreds of people. We had struck a chord and were meeting a real need, but it quickly became clear that the Sunday clinic was simply not adequate to meet the need.

"How Can I Help You?"

We had a little money in the bank, but not nearly enough to get the clinic up and running beyond Sunday morning. We needed start-up funds. We didn't know how it would happen, but we knew it would happen. The clinic would be a reality.

One day I received a call from an old Edgewater High School friend, Curtis Hodges. He said he had heard about what we were doing and wanted to see it. I recalled that Mother Teresa responded to people who wanted to see her medical hospital by saying, "Come and see." I'm no Mother Teresa, and our clinic is not a major hospital, but I definitely believe in the concept of "come and see." (Any charity you can't go and see at any time of the day isn't worth supporting.) I responded to my high school buddy the same way Mother Teresa would have: "Come and see!" We met a few days later, and I could tell from the very beginning that this was going to be memorable. I didn't pressure or poor-mouth him—I never do. I simply let him see, feel, and experience our mission. We walked outside and stood in the parking lot. I should mention, my friend is quite intimidating. He's six-feet-four-inches tall, has a dominant personality, and is hard to read, so I never expected to hear what he said next.

"Scott," he said, "I have everything the world has to offer. I've been blessed." Then he teared up and said, "What do you need me to do for you?"

Normally, when people say this, I play it off and tell them I'll get back to them (as sometimes people say this but really don't mean it). This time, however, I felt bold and courageous and quickly responded, "I need you to build me a clinic."

At first, I couldn't believe what I had said, but after I said it, it felt good—so I said it again! To my amazement, he said, "I'll do it." Boy, did he do it. One hundred and twenty days from that conversation, he mobilized volunteers, vendors, supporters, and contractors, and built a first-class professional medical clinic, with seven exam rooms and an office—fully furnished.

To this day, our clinic is up and running, helping hundreds and hundreds of children and families each year. It was our destiny to fulfill the dream of seeing this become a reality: a medical clinic was born.

A Beyond Ordinary Meeting

Now that the clinic was actually built, it seemed to be a good time to think about how to fund it. Sure, we had things a little backwards, but it seemed to work out. As miraculous as it was to have gotten the clinic built, the initial funding of it was just as amazing.

One night, my wife Tammi was at dinner with several friends on Park Avenue in Winter Park, a beautiful area of parks, restaurants, and shopping. It was a girls' night out, and they were all enjoying a nice evening together. At some point, one of her friends recognized a well-known, popular leader in the Central Florida area, John Morgan. The women approached the man's table and made small talk. Somehow, the conversation turned to what Tammi and her husband did for a living. Since all the women at the table were donors and friends of the outreach, they enthusiastically talked about what we did for our community. They made quite an impression on the man with their genuine passion for what we did, because after the conversation, he simply handed Tammi his card and said: "Have Scott call me. I want to meet him."

Tammi came home that night and tossed the card on the table. "Here— he wants you to call him tomorrow." I get a lot of cards and meet a lot of people who tell me to call them, so this was not uncommon. However, when I saw the name on *this* card, I almost fell out of my chair. The first words out of my mouth were, "You've got to be kidding." I couldn't believe what I was seeing. Then Tammi told me about her encounter with the man and all she and the other women had said and done. It was an incredible story.

It took me days, but I finally worked up the courage to give the man a call. I was surprised to have my call put right through to his office. I spoke with his assistant, who confirmed that he did indeed want to see me. We scheduled a meeting for a few days later.

"I Want to Hear Your Story."

Tammi and I made our way to downtown Orlando, to John Morgan's offices in a high-rise building. After a few minutes in the lobby, we met with him. We were not scared or intimidated. We were confident in the mission we had started, but this was not an ordinary meeting, for sure. It was a big opportunity for us. After exchanging some small talk, he said: "You've got an hour. I want to hear your story." For the next hour, we shared our story. It went very well. I enjoyed the opportunity and was grateful, as always, to share the vision with others. At the close of our meeting, John simply said, "I like what I hear. Give me a few days."

It doesn't matter how big or important or rich or poor they are, I share my passion with people with the same conviction. I have always used this phrase as my motto: "If I go after the people no one wants, God will bring me the people everyone is after." As I remain faithful to the poor and needy, I believe that God will bring me before people who can (and will) help further the mission. That was certainly true in this case.

A few days later, John contacted me and asked that we prepare a proposal for funding the entire clinic with doctors, nurses, staff, and equipment. We complied, and just a few months later, we received word that he had decided to fund the entire clinic. Those without access to medical care—children, teens, their parents, and the elderly—would now receive first-class medical treatment.

All this happened because two men on separate paths came together to unite with the spoken vision. One would build the clinic; the other would fund *all* the operational costs! They touched the heart of God together.

Questions for you on ....
Chapter 5: Do Good, Be Great by Harnessing the Power of Habit

1. When you read about Oprah Winfrey, what are some of the do good, be great qualities you see?

2. Pick out one of the quotes from Oprah Winfrey and discuss why this particular quote inspires you.

3. List out 5 healthy habits that you live everyday and list another 5 habits that you can begin today.

4. How can you begin to develop the habit of compassion in your life?

5. In what ways can you begin today to live a life of generosity?

6. List several ways in which you can offer hope to others.

Notes

Great Quotes from a Great Leader
Gandhi

- *"Where there is love there is life."*
- *"There are people in the world so hungry that God cannot appear to them except in the form of bread."*
- *"Earth provides enough to satisfy every man's needs, but not every man's greed."*
- *"To give pleasure to a single heart by a single act is better than a thousand heads bowing in prayer."*
- *"To deprive a man of his natural liberty and to deny to him the ordinary amenities of life is worse than starving the body; it is starvation of the soul, the dweller in the body."*
- *"You must not lose faith in humanity. Humanity is an ocean; if a few drops of the ocean are dirty, the ocean does not become dirty."*
- *"An eye for an eye only ends up making the whole world blind."*
- *"Gentleness, self-sacrifice, and generosity are the exclusive possession of no one race or religion."*
- *"In prayer, it is better to have a heart without words than words without a heart."*
- *"A life of sacrifice is the pinnacle of art and is full of true joy."*
- *"Poverty is the worst form of violence."*
- *"The best way to find yourself is to lose yourself in the service of others."*

6

Avoiding Toxic Charity by Do Good, Be Great

KEY 6: BEYOND ORDINARY
PEOPLE LIVE LIFE PUTTING FIRST THINGS FIRST

MOHANDAS GANDHI—Do Good, Be Great
for Those Who Are Suppressed

On January 30, 1948, at about 5 o'clock in the afternoon, Mohandas Gandhi was shot to death as he stood outside a building in Delhi, India, where a prayer meeting was to take place. The gunman, a fellow Hindu, fired three times before he was seized by the crowd. He later said he disagreed with Gandhi's theology and was "not sorry at all" for killing the man hailed as the twentieth century's most influential advocate of non-violent change.

As the architect of peaceful civil disobedience, Gandhi crafted an expression of political protest admired and successfully replicated by the century's pioneering civil rights leaders, Nelson Mandela and Dr. Martin Luther King Jr. Because of the legacy he forged in his attempts to do good, be Great, Gandhi is revered as the "father" of modern India—the one who led his country from British colonialism to sovereign independence.

He was born Mohandas Karamchand Gandhi on October 2, 1869, in Porbandar, on the Kathiawar peninsula of India. His father had been prime minister of the state, and the family closely observed official traditions.

Marriage was one, and Gandhi was engaged three times as a child. His first two fiancées died. His third engagement, which occurred when he was only seven, resulted in a marriage at age thirteen that lasted more than sixty years.

His parents wanted him to be a lawyer, and at age nineteen he went to England to study law at the University College London. Three years later, he returned to India and tried to start his own law practice but was unsuccessful. He opted for a job with an Indian firm and moved to South Africa in 1893 to work out of its Durban office.

There, he was appalled by the mistreatment of Indian immigrants and joined a struggle to secure their basic civil rights. In 1906, after an ordinance passed regarding the registration of Indians, Gandhi led a campaign of civil disobedience that lasted the next eight years. In 1913, hundreds of Indians living in South Africa, women included, were jailed, and thousands of striking Indian miners were imprisoned and flogged, or shot. Pressured by Britain and India alike, South Africa accepted a compromise negotiated by Gandhi that included a number of important concessions, such as the recognition of Indian marriages.

During the twenty years Gandhi lived in South Africa, he was imprisoned several times—though not without also achieving some of his goals. In 1914 the government conceded to many of his demands for immigrants' rights. It was in South Africa that he developed his *satyagraha*, or "devotion to truth"—a new nonviolent way to right sociopolitical wrongs. It was the approach he would practice throughout his life.

Returning to India in 1919, Gandhi became president of the Indian National Congress, one of the two major political parties in the country. He began to lead the fight for Indian independence from Britain by organizing large, nonviolent civil disobedience campaigns to protest injustices in national labor practices, the courts, and other areas.

His campaigns of peaceful noncooperation with the British led to thousands of arrests, however, and he backed off when violence ensued. During one protest, British troops killed 379 unarmed demonstrators who had gathered in a city park. It marked a political turning point for Gandhi.

Whereas his support had been behind only partial autonomy for his country, after the massacre, he became convinced that India should accept nothing less than total independence from Britain.

Gandhi was jailed numerous times for organizing the protests and often would undertake long fasts during his incarceration. Fearing the Indian masses which had grown to love Gandhi, the British government often shortened his prison terms, lest he die in prison and civil unrest break out across the country.

By 1920 he had become a leading figure in Indian politics. However, he withdrew from the public eye for a period during the 1920s, reappearing in 1930 when he organized a new protest to target a British tax on salt. The effort became one of his best known acts of civil disobedience, when he led thousands of Indians on a 241-mile "March to the Sea" to symbolically make their own salt from seawater.

In 1934, Gandhi resigned his leadership of the Indian National Congress and was replaced by Jawaharlal Nehru. In 1945, the British government began negotiations that led to the Mountbatten Plan two years later, which called for India and Pakistan to be created as independent states divided along religious lines. Gandhi, openly breaking with the Congress party, opposed the Hindu-Muslim division. He staunchly believed that the British must leave and let India work out its own fate.

Violence erupted when the British plan was implemented, leading to a staggering loss of life. Estimates (which vary widely) claim that between 200,000 and 1 million Hindus, Sikhs, and Muslims were killed. Gandhi fasted in an attempt to establish peace.

On August 15, 1947, India finally gained full independence from Britain. Viceroy Louis Mountbatten, for whom the plan was named (and who administered the transfer of power from England), praised Gandhi as the "architect of India's freedom through nonviolence."

Seven months later, Gandhi was dead. He had fought most of his life for the dignity of others. His compassion for humanity, dedication to social equity, and passion for justice had brought sustainable change to his beloved India. It was now a sovereign state that would speak for itself.

Gandhi had also become a saint in the eyes of millions of his countrymen, who anointed him *Mahatma*, or, "the great-souled one"—an appellation that continues to this day.

"Nonviolence," he said, "is the greatest force at the disposal of mankind. It is mightier than the mightiest weapon of destruction devised by the ingenuity of man."

On the evening of Gandhi's assassination, Nehru, who had ascended to the office of prime minister, announced in a radio address heard across India: "Gandhi has gone out of our lives. The father of our nation is no more."

If anyone ever confronted dysfunction and a broken system in India, it was Gandhi. He was familiar with the flawed attitudes and actions of those who didn't want liberty and freedom. Today, much like in Gandhi's India, there are forces content with the old traditional ways of helping people out of poverty. Although some aspects of traditional charity have been time-tested over the years, real change and help will be achieved when we adopt new strategies and methodologies that embrace self-sufficiency as the ultimate goal.

Toxic—*Acting as or having the effect of a poison; poisonous.*

Toxic Encounter
Toxic Charity Poisons Everyone
Dozens of volunteers were prepping the canned goods to be given away for the weekly food giveaway. The room was filled with joy and excitement as they made preparations for the needy families who would come to the church to receive food. A pallet of groceries had been purchased from a local food bank, and the food was being cleaned and sorted by volunteers. Each bag was carefully packed with all the necessary ingredients, including cereal, snacks, canned goods, and occasionally, a bag of candy for good measure.

After an hour of prep work, the team of dedicated church members gathered a few minutes before 7 p.m. to pray. The prayer was sincere and heartfelt. The volunteers asked for God's blessing on the evening and prayed that each person who would come that evening would feel God's presence and love. They ended the prayer by thanking God for the opportunity, and for His blessing on each person. The prayer ended with a joyous, "And all God's people said, *Amen!*" Everyone had gathered in a circle and placed their hands on top of one another's, much like basketball players when they gather together with their coach before tip-off. They even counted aloud together, "1, 2, 3, *break!*" before they dispersed to their different posts for the evening.

Some volunteers went to their posts as greeters, some filled out paperwork, some handed out bags, and others carried the food outside to cars. Up to that point, their efforts and the work they were doing were healthy and happy, but it soon turned toxic and poisonous, and no one saw it coming—not even me.

It was about a half hour into the weekly event that things went south quickly after a certain family arrived. We had seen them before. They had visited several times and were what we called "a regular."

Every other family we served that evening was appreciative and thankful. They didn't seem to expect special treatment; they were just in a tough spot and appreciated the assistance. They were even receptive to prayer when offered by volunteers who wanted to take a few minutes to not only feed their bodies, but encourage their spirits as well.

However, this one family seemed to bring a toxic vibe into the kitchen that night. The "mother" didn't say much, but you could tell she had done this before. This wasn't her first "rodeo," and she knew the routine better than most of our volunteers. She came with an attitude of entitlement and privilege. It wasn't what she said—it was how she acted. She took several of our volunteers by surprise.

It didn't help that she had gotten out of a luxury SUV parked out front, or that she had a male companion who looked ashamed to get out of the car with her. (He waited in the car and talked on his cell phone while the woman came in for the handout.) As I observed all this, I hoped the volunteers were as perceptive as I was. (Yes, they had noticed, I saw.) They spotted the designer purse the woman carried and the fancy jeans she wore.

They noticed that she demanded food without appreciation, gratitude, or an attempt at relationship.

I could feel the tension rising in the room as I watched her interact with volunteers. It wasn't going well, but at least the volunteers' eyes were being opened to the complexity that can come when doing good.

Suddenly the woman very rudely blurted out to the front desk volunteers: "Y'all ain't got any meat!"

Quickly the atmosphere in the room shifted from joy, excitement, and happiness to frustration and disappointment. The volunteers tried to explain that we didn't offer meat. They apologized and offered a few extra cans of vegetables and fruit to try to please her. But their attempts were futile. Hoping that a final prayer would change the atmosphere, a few volunteers mustered up enough grace to say grace and asked her if they could pray for her. Several volunteers gathered around her, and one placed a hand on the woman's shoulder to try to make a connection of some kind.

As the volunteers prayed, I decided to pray with my eyes open. I wanted to observe and I hoped that God wouldn't mind. (Most of the time I pray with eyes closed, and I've always taught my children as we pray at dinnertime to bow their heads to offer thanks.) I could see that the woman was looking up; she appeared uninterested, unengaged, and unmoved. She was totally going through the motions, knowing she had to endure this hardship for only a few more seconds and then she would finally get what she came for—free food. She was savvy enough to close her eyes for the final sentence of the prayer and the final amen. I'm glad the faithful volunteers didn't see what I had seen; and the prayer time thankfully seemed to calm the tension in the room.

Then, like clockwork, the woman finished the transaction. She knew what would happen next: A few bags of food were handed to her and a hearty "God bless you!" expressed by the volunteers. It all took just a few seconds; however, that interaction would last a lifetime.

Having done this a few times as a pastor and nonprofit leader, I knew it would be best to just end this encounter as quickly as possible for her benefit and that of the volunteers. I offered to carry out the few bags of food to the waiting car and to hopefully put this appointment behind us, and she accepted. The walk from the church kitchen was only a few feet, but it felt like it lasted an eternity.

"Do you realize all the effort we have put into this? Why are you so ungrateful?" Those and a few other questions raced through my mind, but I maintained my composure and refrained from losing my cool. I hoped my silence would give her one last chance to salvage the evening. I prayed she would say something to me that would change the way I felt and how the volunteers felt. Down deep, I wanted this to end differently so I could go back into the church and rescue the situation. Nothing was said, but much had been communicated.

As I reached her car to place the few bags of food inside (with no help from her male companion), I quickly observed that the car was filled with banana boxes—the most common form of packaging used by food banks when distributing groceries. Our kitchen obviously wasn't the first or last stop for this couple. They clearly had made the rounds to other churches and charities that evening. Their car was full of free food, and my heart and the hearts of our dedicated volunteers were empty.

That night changed the way I viewed poverty, compassion, and handouts. That bitter taste of one-way giving and toxic charity were enough for me. As a result, I changed our approach and helped pioneer a healthy way of helping people in need.

I wish I could tell you this encounter was the exception, but the reality for me and many others in the nonprofit world is that this type of interaction has become normal, even the rule. We've allowed it and encouraged it, and it has had a negative impact on those we serve, on our volunteers, on our donors, and ultimately, on the leaders of nonprofits.

"I am for doing good to the poor, but I differ in opinion of the means. I think the best way of doing good to the poor, is not making them easy in poverty, but leading or driving them out of it." (Benjamin Franklin)

Do Good, Be Great by Leading People Out of Poverty

When I first read this painful and profound statement by Benjamin Franklin, frankly, I did not understand it, was offended by it, and I disagreed with it wholeheartedly. Twenty years later, I now look back at his statement and humbly confess that I get it. In fact, I applaud it and agree 110 percent with what he said.

Benjamin Franklin is renowned for being full of wisdom and knowledge; people all over the world quote him and use his wise words. Yet I've never ever heard anyone use this quote before, especially not in the nonprofit world. In our quest for do good, be Great, we must come to the place where we address the issue of entitlement and giving—not handouts but a hand up.

In my early years of working in the nonprofit world, I was perplexed by how many nonprofits and their leaders were so passionate about helping people yet content with leaving them in poverty. They had no desire to lead them out of it! For the last twenty years, I have totally embraced the "hand up" model, which advocates practical steps to get people out of poverty. It says that, as nonprofit leaders, our goal should be to provide a way out, not keep people imprisoned in poverty. Many organizations are content simply with helping people, not moving them forward, and certainly not toward healthy self-sufficiency.

Several years ago, I was asked to serve on a committee to address nonprofit work in the state of Florida. After several very long meetings, I settled in and became comfortable with sharing some of my ideas and philosophies. I thought they would inspire and motivate the other members as we discussed people in poverty and entitlement attitudes. Boy, was I wrong. My comments were quickly dismissed and rejected. During a break, other members of the committee said something to me I will never forget: "Mr. George, you are idealistic and you are pushing the envelope a bit too much. We are quite satisfied with our current model and don't anticipate changing anytime in the near future."

As we pursue to do good, be Great, I believe it is healthy to take a close look at why we do good, how we do good, and what we can do to improve to the point of do good, be Great. We don't want our help to *hurt*; we want it to *help*!

Could it be that *your* help may be hurting your cause? We'll look at a few ways your help can hurt your efforts and offer some ideas to make sure your helping is helping.

9 Ways to Know if Your Helping Is Hurting

1. *One-way Giving Is Embraced and Celebrated*

One-way giving is the traditional approach to charity. Giving is limited to one direction, from the giver to those in need. There is no reciprocity. This is an imbalanced approach and model. When you embrace one-way giving, you create an unhealthy relationship that is imbalanced and not sustainable. The key to moving people out of poverty to sustainability is to form a healthy relationship in which both parties are committed and mutually give to make the relationship stronger.

In one-way giving, the giver becomes discouraged and fatigued, and the recipient develops an attitude of entitlement. In any healthy relationship, there is reciprocal give-and-take. Each party benefits in the relationship. Why should charity work be the only sector that does not expect two-way giving and receiving?

Two-way Giving: Healthy Charity at Its Best

Sandra was once happily married with three children. Life was good until divorce crept into it and brought devastation to her relationship with her husband and children. She heard that she could find a job in Central Florida, so she set off from the Northeast to the Sunshine State, looking for a fresh start and a new lease on life. Friends who encouraged her to come to Florida to find work were right about her being able to find a job here. What they didn't know was that the pay was only $7.50 per hour, so Sandra quickly had to find two jobs to simply survive. She worked day and night as a single parent trying her best to provide for her family. She also had to provide emotional strength for her teenage children during the difficult transition.

Sandra's childhood dream was to become a nurse, but she realized it wasn't the best time for her to take on another project, much less night school. But she did it and went to school at night at one of the local hospitals in downtown Orlando. Sandra needed a hand up. She was fighting against the tide and needed a place where she could get a little help, hope, and encouragement. She was looking for a partner charity that would come alongside her and give her a hand. But she also understood that it wouldn't be a one-way street; in order for the partnership to work, it would involve give-and-take, yin and yang.

She knew it would involve mutual accountability and responsibility. Giving back to the organization would mean volunteering what little time she had. She would come down and offer a bit of help. In turn, she would come and shop at our cost-share grocery program each week. She would visit with our crisis staff for advice and insight on how to get through her transition, tuck some money away, and cut expenses. She attended classes and bettered herself. It wasn't easy and most people would have given up. For years, she would come to our campus, say hello to the staff, and peek into my office to say hi and give me an update on her schooling, her children, and her future. Her situation wasn't pretty, but poverty isn't pretty and divorce isn't pretty—at times, life isn't pretty. Sandra never asked for a handout. She never expected special treatment, and certainly didn't have an entitlement mentality. She wasn't looking for pity, but partnership. Many times in life, you get out of a relationship what you put into it. She invested and gave, and she received in reciprocal fashion.

Several months went by, and I made a mental note that she hadn't peeked her head into my office in a while. You can imagine that with more than 500 families a day coming to our campus, one might easily lose track of people, but I often think of them and wonder how they are doing. Did they make it? Are they self-sufficient? Could we have done more to really help people with a hand up? Did they fall back into extreme poverty and hopelessness? I wondered about Sandra a few times and should have reached out, but didn't. There would have always been a question in the back of my mind about whether she was a success or failure if she hadn't stepped back into the office one day.

In an instant, I knew she was a success. Her face was bright and her eyes were filled with life and inner peace. She was confident and full of optimism. She was a different person. It didn't take but a few seconds to realize her life had been turned around in a big way and that she was filled with appreciation and gratitude. She proceeded to fill me in. The details included graduation from nursing school, a full-time job at one of the major hospitals in Orlando, a new marriage, and her children excelling in school and community involvement. Then she dropped the bomb on me—I mean in a good way.

She told me how thankful she was for our staff and the programs we offered her in her darkest moments. With a tear in her eye, she told me that for months she had been looking for a way to give back—to say thank you. She then told me her son was working on his Eagle Scout rank with the Boy Scouts of America, and that as a family they had decided to adopt our charity as his project. They planned to hold several community and neighborhood food drives to help us continue to help other families just like theirs.

Several weeks went by, and we had arranged for the food to be delivered into our pantry on a Saturday afternoon. Sandra made sure all her children and her new husband were present when the truckload of food was delivered. Their smiles and the joy on each of their faces were priceless. They matched the smile on my face and the joy in my heart for another family rescued. One more family was dedicated to two-way giving and healthy restoration—a bond in which both the donor and recipient have dignity, relationship, and partnership.

Poverty is a difficult force to conquer. Sandra and her family showed me that when both sides have skin in the game and are committed to two-way giving and healthy restoration, the rate of moving people out of poverty into self-sufficiency is much higher.

2. Handouts Are the Only Option for Helping

For many years, I was under the impression that handouts were the only model for helping people. After all, that was what others had always modeled for me. If someone needs something, you hand it out to them; no questions asked, no long-term game plan in place, and no strategy for self-sufficiency. There are times when handouts are needed, but it took fifteen years before I saw a new model emerge that both intrigued me and changed my idea of how best to help people—a hand up.

It is partnership that leads to self-sufficiency, just like what we saw in Sandra's story. I have used the following model to see thousands of families move from handout to self-sufficiency:

Give Them a Hand

Hand out—relief: This stage provides emergency relief for people in situational poverty.

Hand held—recover: This stage begins to stabilize people and is the first step in a strategy of sustainability.

Hand stand—restore: At this stage, the person in poverty begins to take personal responsibility for breaking the cycle of poverty. He or she begins to stand on his or her own.

Hand up—rehabilitate: This stage embraces partnership between those in poverty and those who walk with them, hand in hand.

Hand off—release: In this stage, the person in poverty has begun to apply what he or she has learned and walks on his or her own.

Hand clap—rejoice: This stage celebrates the conclusion of the entire process of moving people from poverty to self-sustainability.

3. Relationships Are Broken

In *When Helping Hurts,* authors Steve Corbel and Brian Fikkert clearly identify the issue of broken relationships:

If we think poverty is lack of resource, then we focus on building ministries that try to get more resources. If we think poverty is lack of education, then we try to get someone more education. Poverty is the result of broken relationships.

Our relationship to God is broken resulting in broken fears and misunderstandings.
Our relationship to others is broken resulting in broken blame and using others.
Our relationship to ourselves is broken resulting in broken shame and self esteem.
Our relationship to the world is broken resulting in lack of resources and jobs.[17]

People in poverty need healthy and whole relationships. They need people who are committed to a long-term, sustainable, relationship-filled community that will steadily see the cycle of poverty broken off their lives.

4. *Entitlement Is the End Result*
Bob Lupton, author of *Toxic Charity* has used his years of helping in the inner city of Atlanta to uncover the following unhealthy, slippery slope that many charities and nonprofits fall into:

Entitlement vs. Empowerment
Give once and you elicit appreciation
Give twice and you create anticipation
Give three times and you create expectation
Give four times and it becomes entitlement
Give five times and you establish dependency. [18]

Entitlement is defined by Webster as, "the condition of having a right to have, do, or get something," and, "the feeling or right that you deserve to be given something." When did this type of attitude creep into our models on nonprofit/charity?

Is it a right or a responsibility to help someone or give a needy family assistance? For some time, the nonprofit world has embraced the belief that the needy have the right to be helped. I say it's not a right! Real change will happen when we move away from the "entitlement attitude" of "This is my right!" to the belief that some people in need have a responsibility to be a part of the solution. They need to move into an empowerment philosophy.

Empowerment is defined, "to give power to someone, to give official authority/power to others." If we are going to see real change and transformation in our communities, we'd better change the way we think and move from entitlement to empowerment.

I can tell you who's ready to make this change from right to responsibility—donors! Donors are generous people who don't mind giving to a need, but the ones in our community have what I call "donor fatigue." People work very hard for the things they possess. They are weary of giving their hard-earned money to people who have a mentality that they have a right to have or get.

Entitlement doesn't work! It doesn't work in government, it doesn't work in church, and it doesn't work in charity. Toxic charity produces entitlement; healthy charity produces empowerment. Toxic charity is handouts; healthy charity is a hand up. The focus of toxic charity is, "What I can get from you?" A healthy charity focus is, "What can we accomplish together?" Toxic charity fatigues the donor, while healthy charity energizes the giver to continue giving. Toxic charity produces enablement, while healthy charity produces self-sufficiency. Toxic charity is emergency relief focused, while healthy charity is development focused.

5. Self-Sufficiency Is Ignored
Hand Up Philosophy: A Hand Up, Not a Handout (Beyond Ordinary Approach)

To meet the needs of hurting families in need of food assistance and help, we knew we didn't want to duplicate what other churches and nonprofit centers were doing. We wanted to go beyond ordinary. Most of the families that flocked to our church were not homeless. In fact, most of them were working families, with moms or dads who often worked two jobs, but they were still unable to make ends meet. These families were not asking for handouts. They wanted a hand up.

This model would build dignity and responsibility in people so that both donor and recipient would feel good about it.

For thousands of years, the Jewish people have used the Maimonides model for helping people and restoring dignity. The "Levels of Tzedakah" ("levels of charity") restores the dignity of the poor while keeping the goal of self-sufficiency in sight.

The Levels of Tzedakah (Highest to Lowest)

Enabling the recipient to become self-reliant
Giving when neither party knows the other's identity
Giving when one knows the recipient's identity, but the recipient doesn't know the donor's identity
Giving when one does not know the recipient's identity, but the recipient knows the identity of the donor
Giving before being asked
Giving after being asked
Giving less than one should, but giving it cheerfully
Giving begrudgingly
- Moses Maimonides, Philosopher

Destiny Community Assistance Center Is Born

In the summer of 2001, we made plans to begin implementing this innovative model of assistance. This beyond ordinary approach took months to fine-tune and develop, but we owe much to the Habitat for Humanity nonprofit model. They do not simply give homes away to families in need, but partner with them to work toward finding affordable housing. Poor working families have to apply themselves and expend considerable "sweat equity" toward the goal of home ownership. I remember thinking, *If they can pioneer this model with homes, why can't we use it with food?* We would not simply give away food all the time. We would develop a model by which working families in need would partner with us, and we would make affordable food available for purchase, and help move families from poverty to self-sustainability.

6. No Plan in Place for Real Transformation

When you desire to do good, and be Great you have to have a long-term plan in place to see the people you are serving break the cycle of poverty. In developing our hand up model, we used the following questions to keep us on track.

1. What do I want the future to look like for those I'm helping?

Vision is a picture held in your mind's eye of the way things could or should be in the days ahead. Vision connotes a visual reality, a portrait of a preferred future. The picture is internal and personal.

You will be able to accomplish your vision only after you've painted it on the canvas of your mind. You must define the dream clearly and compellingly before you pursue it. As Michael Hyatt observes, "If the vision is not clear, no strategy will work, and it will be impossible to prioritize correctly." Most people skip the step of clarifying their vision, and their dream remains fuzzy and unspecific. As a result, they never achieve it.

2. How do I move the people I'm helping to a goal of self-sufficiency?

Fulfilling your vision means you have to stop stargazing. People who see their vision materialize are the ones who have devised concrete plans to enlist supporters, gather resources, and upgrade their abilities. By translating a lengthy journey into smaller steps, and by creating mile markers to chart progress, a strategy inspires action.

3. Am I using my time wisely when helping others?

Time cannot be managed. It cannot be controlled in any way. It marches on no matter what you do, like a taxi meter that keeps running whether you are moving or standing still. Everyone gets the same number of hours and minutes in a day. Nobody—no matter how shrewd—can save minutes from one day to spend on another. People talk about trying to find time, but they need to quit looking. There aren't any extra minutes lying around.

Since you can't manage your time, what can you do? Manage yourself! Nothing separates successful people from unsuccessful people more than how they use their time. Successful people understand that time is the most precious commodity on earth. As a result, they know where their time goes. They continually analyze how they are using their time and ask themselves the question, "Am I getting the best use out of my time?"[19]

7. Partners Are Not Embraced

Poverty is complicated and difficult. No one has a corner on the market when it comes to helping people out of poverty. There are others who can help you do good, be Great, and the sooner you realize that you need others and others need you, the better off you and the people you are helping will be.

There are too many churches and charities operating in a "solo" philosophy. The strength of an organization is determined by how many influences it has in its life to accomplish its mission. Be open to embrace others to help you accomplish your dreams and execute your mission.

8. The "Oath for Compassion" Is Abandoned
Oath for Compassionate Service

- Never do for the poor what the poor have (or could have) the capacity to do for themselves.
- Limit one-way giving to emergency situations.
- Strive to empower the poor through employment, leading, investing, using give-outs sparingly to ensure achievements.
- Subordinate self-interests to the needs of those being served.
- Listen closely to those you seek to help, especially to what is not being said—unspoken feelings may contain essential clues to effective service.
- Above all, do no harm. [20]

9. *Emergency Relief Is Highlighted Above Development Relief*
When Justice and Mercy Meet

Bob Lupton, the author of *Toxic Charity*, indicates that the Bible places equal emphasis on mercy and justice:

> *Most of our current charity focuses primarily on emergency relief. Emergency relief is necessary, but developmental relief is the long-term solution. If you want your efforts to really bring the desired results, then developmental relief must be embraced.*
>
> *This approach and mindset is demonstrated best in the Bible. There are many instances when giving to the poor is admonished, but there are also times when "be kind to the poor" is also taught.*
>
> **Giving** *to the poor is "emergency relief."* **Being kind** *to the poor may be viewed as "development relief."*
>
> *I believe it is critical for charities, churches, and nonprofits to adopt both approaches as they desire to bring holistic help to those in need. This one-two approach is also demonstrated in the popular verse from Micah 6:8 (NIV): "He has shown you, O mortal, what is good. And what does the Lord require of you? To act justly and to love mercy and to walk humbly with your God."*
>
> *With this concept in mind, the one-two example is clear: act justly/love mercy. If we take this philosophy a step further, act justly could mean "developmental relief" and* **love mercy** *could mean "emergency relief." It's not either or—it's both.* [21]

Bob Lupton breaks this down:

- **Act justly**... *Justice is fairness or reasonableness, especially in the way people are treated or decisions are made.*
- **Love mercy**... *Mercy is compassion, kindness, or forgiveness shown especially to someone over whom a person has power.*

Joined together, these commands lead us to "holistic involvement." Divorced, they become deformed. Mercy without justice degenerates into dependency and entitlement, preserving the power of the giver over the recipient. Justice without mercy is cold and impersonal; more concerned about rights than relationships. The addict needs both food and treatment. The young woman needs both a safe place to sleep and a way out of her entrapping lifestyle. Street kids need both friendship and jobs. Mercy combined with justice creates:

- *immediate care with a future plan*
- *emergency relief and responsible development*
- *short-term intervention and long-term involvement*
- *heart responses and engaged minds*

Mercy is a door, an opening, an invitation to touch a life, to make a difference. But it is not a destination." [22]

Questions for you on ....
Chapter 6: Avoiding Toxic Charity by Do Good, Be Great

1. When you read about Mohandas Gandhi, what are some of the do good be great qualities you see?

2. Pick out one of the quotes from Mohandas Gandhi and discuss why this particular quote inspires you.

3. How does this quote from Benjamin Franklin challenge your idea of people in poverty?

   "I am for doing good to the poor, but I differ in opinion of the means. I think the best way of doing good to the poor, is not making them easy in poverty, but leading or driving them out of it."

4. What does toxic charity look like to you?

5. Have you ever experienced toxic charity? Describe it. How does it make you feel?

6. Two-way giving...what does it look like to you? How can you change one-way into two-way giving?

Notes

Great Quotes from a Great Leader
Bill Gates

- *"Is the rich world aware of how 4 billion of the 6 billion live? If we were aware, we would want to help out, we'd want to get involved."*
- *"The general idea of the rich helping the poor, I think, is important."*
- *"Until we're educating every kid in a fantastic way, until every inner city is cleaned, there is no shortage of things to do."*
- *"I realized ten years ago that my wealth has to go back to society. A fortune, the size of which is hard to imagine, is best not passed on to one's children. It's not constructive for them."*
- *"We make the future sustainable when we invest in the poor, not when we insist on their suffering."*
- *"Although I don't have a prescription for what others should do, I know I have been very fortunate and feel a responsibility to give back to society in a very significant way."*
- *"Investing for the poor requires participation from the entire community."*

7

Do Good, Be Great With Integrity Guardrails

KEY 7: BEYOND ORDINARY PEOPLE LIVE
WITH INTEGRITY GUARDRAILS

BILL GATES—Do Good, Be Great for Those Who Need a Hand Up

William Henry Gates III, cofounder of the Microsoft Corporation, was born in Seattle, Washington, on October 28, 1955. He is the middle child of prominent Seattle lawyer William H. Gates II and schoolteacher Mary Gates, and has two siblings: Kristi, the oldest, and Libby.

Probably due to the brash brilliance he would manifest later in his life, Gates grew bored easily with school as a child and ended up getting into a lot of trouble. At age thirteen, his parents sent him to Lakeside Preparatory School with the hope that it would present more of an educational challenge for young Bill. Whether it did or not, Lakeside was where the seedlings of his greatness and amazing future sprouted.

It was there he wrote his first software program at age thirteen. In high school he helped form a group of programmers who computerized the school's payroll system. They also founded a company called Traf-O-Data that sold traffic-counting systems to local governments. Most important, Lakeside was where Gates met fellow student Paul Allen, with whom he would create a startup company in college called Microsoft.

Scoring 1590 out of 1600 on his SAT, Gates enrolled at Harvard in 1973. Soon he was a regular at the nightly poker games in his residence hall. He would win or lose hundreds of dollars in a night—and he eventually lost thousands. But the experience taught him how to bluff, a skill he would put to good use in a life-changing business transaction only a year later.

In 1974, after seeing a magazine ad for a new microcomputer called the Altair 8080, Gates and Allen thought they could adapt the programming language BASIC for the Altair. At the time, BASIC was a mainframe-only software.

At Gates' request, Allen called Ed Roberts, CEO of the company that made the Altair, to tell him they had a microcomputer version of BASIC almost finished. They were bluffing, and Roberts called their bluff. But he conceded that whoever delivered a working version of BASIC first would get the Altair contract—no matter who they were. Gates and Allen burned the midnight oil for two months. When Allen presented their version of the software to Roberts, their gamble paid off, and they won the deal. Gates would later say, "Business is a money game with few rules and a lot of risk."

After Altair, Gates and Allen never looked back. The next year, Gates dropped out of Harvard to start Microsoft, or "Micro-soft" as the name originally appeared—a combination of "microcomputer" and "software." Though he commanded only a small, fledgling company, Gates kept a big eye on Japan, where micro computing was exploding in the late seventies. In 1979, he won a major Japanese contract which led to many business trips to Japan, and more contracts.

In 1980, however, he struck a deal with US-based IBM that revolutionized the computing world. Microsoft would provide the MS-DOS operating system on the new IBM Personal Computer (PC). Gates sold the software to IBM for $50,000, but retained the all-important copyright. When the PC market exploded, thanks to its copyright, Microsoft sold MS-DOS to PC manufacturers worldwide.

In 1985, Gates released the Microsoft Windows operating system (OS) to answer a similar system introduced by Apple Computers in 1984. Because Windows could run on a variety of PC-compatible machines, unlike the Apple OS, Microsoft won the battle, and soon Windows was installed on about 90 percent of the world's PCs.

The next year, Gates took Microsoft public with stock worth $520 million. Continued rapid growth raised the value of Gates' personal stock to $100 billion. He was, and still is, the richest person in the world, according to the 2015 *Forbes* Billionaires List, which values his fortune at $79 billion.

Today, however, Gates is heralded not as often for his personal computing as for his personal philanthropy. Challenged by his wife, Melinda, to give his wealth to charity, in 1994 he founded the William H. Gates Foundation with her in 1994. In 1999, the foundation was renamed the Bill and Melinda Gates Foundation. Its mission is to work with partner organizations worldwide in tackling critical problems that fall into the foundation's four purpose areas:

1. **Global Development Division:** to help the world's poorest people lift themselves out of hunger and poverty.
2. **Global Health Division:** to harness advances in science and technology to save lives in developing countries.
3. **US Division:** to improve high school and post-secondary education and support vulnerable children and families in Washington state.
4. **Global Policy & Advocacy Division:** to build strategic relationships and promote policies that will advance the vision. In practice, the foundation funds ideas that: (1) help farmers in developing countries to grow more food and earn more money; (2) create new tools to prevent and treat deadly diseases; and (3) pioneer new methods to help students and teachers in the classroom. Gates believes the leadership model emerging today will ultimately replace *managing* people with *empowering* them. "As we look to the twenty-first century, leaders will be those who empower others," Gates says.

Still the quintessential risk taker, Gates believes a key role of philanthropy is to attempt to provide promising solutions that governments and businesses can't afford to take. Today the couple's foundation is one of the largest charitable organizations in the world. Gates himself has donated more than $28 billion.

In 2008 Gates relinquished his day-to-day oversight of Microsoft, but remained chairman of the board. In 2014, he stepped down as chairman. Serving in 2015 as the company's technology advisor, he is no less the unquenchable visionary he has been the last forty years.

Ironically, his philanthropic vision to bring hope, change, and a future for others is driven more by his heart than his gifted mind. Perhaps time and experience have taught him that it is the heart that holds the greatest power to do good, be Great.

I. Do Good, Be Great with Great Character

Microsoft . . . you hear the words and your mind immediately thinks of Bill Gates, his influence, and software and systems that have impacted hundreds of millions of people worldwide. His wealth is unmatched in the world, and so is his integrity and character. His commitment to give most of his fortune away to fight poverty, sickness, and disease should give you an insight into that character, integrity, and his heart. He was obviously brought up with the belief that in the end, all you really have is your character. In our attempt to do good, be Great, character and integrity rank very high in the attitudes that make a person who he or she really is.

D. L. Moody once said, "Character is what you are in the dark when no one is looking." Those who aspire to live beyond ordinary lives must be the same person in the light as they are in the dark. Possessing this quality makes one wealthy, but you don't have to have the fortunes of Bill Gates to be a rich person.

What Is Character?

Let's take a look at what character really is and how we can develop "guardrails"—healthy boundaries—we can set in place to protect us from crashing and burning as we journey through life. I love what Coach John Wooden says in *Coach Wooden's Greatest Secret:*

1. Character is much more than merely being honest.
2. Most of us give ourselves more credit for character than we deserve.
3. You should never mistake your reputation for your character. Be more concerned with your character than your reputation, because your character is what you really are; your reputation is merely what others think you are.
4. Character is formed through the hundreds, if not thousands, of tiny decisions you make throughout each day.[23]

In her bestseller, *What Is a Family?* Edith Schaeffer devotes her longest chapter to the idea that a family is a "perpetual relay of truth." It's a place "where principles are hammered and honed on the anvil of everyday living. Where character traits are sculpted under the watchful eyes of moms and dads. Where steel-strong fibers are woven into the fabric of inner constitution."

The relay race. A race with a hundred batons.

- *Determination.* "Stick with it, regardless."
- *Honesty.* "Speak and live the truth—always."
- *Responsibility.* "Be dependable, be trustworthy."
- *Thoughtfulness.* "Think of others before yourself."
- *Confidentiality.* "Don't tell secrets. Seal your lips."
- *Punctuality.* "Be on time."
- *Self-control.* "When under stress, stay calm."
- *Patience.* "Fight irritability. Be willing to wait."
- *Purity.* "Reject anything that lowers your standards."
- *Compassion.* "When another hurts, feel it with him."
- *Diligence.* "Work hard. Tough it out."[24]

Character Matters

Let's discuss matters that really count when it comes to character. These simple statements will keep you on the straight and narrow:

1. Model it consistently.
2. Speak it continually.
3. Live it daily.
4. Exemplify it humbly.
5. Embrace it wholly.
6. Walk it faithfully.
7. Demonstrate it courageously.
8. Handle it carefully.

Sara Lee Corporation CEO Brenda Barnes says: "The most important thing about leadership is your character and the values that guide your life." She adds: "If you are guided by an internal compass that represents your character and the values that guide your decisions, you're going to be fine. Let your values guide your actions and don't ever lose your internal compass, because everything isn't black or white. There are a lot of gray areas in business."[25]

Character Tests
Just mention the word "test" and people of all ages stress out. You quickly see the fear in their eyes. Whether it's a math test at school or a driving test for one's driver's license, "test" has a negative tone and elicits a fearful reaction from many. When it comes to character and integrity, there are several tests we can take that are not painful and help us stay away from danger. Take the following short test series. It will help you stay in the middle of the road as you travel through life and protect you from going through guardrails and wrecking your marriage, career, or relationships.

1. **Friend Test**: Take a close look at those with whom you associate. Your friends are a reflection of you. Make sure your friends are full of integrity.
2. **Mirror Test**: Look in the mirror and ask yourself the tough questions. Your integrity is dependent on your being able to look at yourself and approve of your actions.

3. **Reputation Test:** Do your walk, your talk, and your actions line up with your reputation? Are you really the person you project to others?

4. **Darkness Test:** What are you doing in the dark? One day the actions done in the dark will come to light. Make sure there are no little areas that you don't want people to see.

5. **Action Test:** Do your actions line up with your talk? Are you practicing what you preach? Actions speak louder than words.

6. **Weakness Test:** In what areas of your life are you most vulnerable? Are you aware of the areas in which you may need accountability?

7. **Choice Test:** Every little choice turns into the sum parts of your integrity. Choose wisely and you will enjoy a lifetime of character.

8. **Isolation Test:** No man is an island. Be sure you are not isolated without friends and associates with whom you can talk and share your heart.

Integrity is the same the world over. It doesn't matter where you were born or what country you live in, integrity and character are universal. People who desire to do good, be Great realize that their character is the same in Russia as it is in Asia or South America.

What Is the Difference Between Image and Integrity?

Psychologist William James wrote a century ago: "I have often thought that the best way to define a man's character is to seek out the particular mental or moral attitude in which . . . he felt himself most deeply and intensively active and alive. At such moments, there is a voice inside which speaks and says, 'This is the real me.'"

(William James, 1842–1910, The Letters of William James)

Many people, when they begin to develop the necessary guardrails to keep them safely on the road, will confuse image and integrity. Let's look at the differences:

1. *Image* is what we appear to be; *Integrity* is who we are.
2. *Image* is actual appearance; *Integrity* is inward beauty.
3. *Image* is the picture; *Integrity* is the face.
4. *Image* is what we want people to see; *Integrity* is what we really are.
5. *Image* happens from the outside; *Integrity* comes from within.
6. *Image* is flashy; *Integrity* is solid.
7. *Image* is what you come with; *Integrity* is what you leave with.
8. *Image* can be learned; *Integrity* must be developed.
9. *Image* is superficial; *Integrity* is the core.
10. *Image* is what people think of you; *Integrity* is what you know you are.
11. *Image* is what others say about you; *Integrity* is what you say about yourself.
12. *Image* is what you are in public; *Integrity* is what you are in the dark. [26]

Leo Rangell, M.D., a psychiatrist and author, explored what he called "the compromise of integrity" in his careful, articulate analysis of the inner workings in the mind and psyche of President Richard M. Nixon and several of his closest confidants related to the Watergate burglary and subsequent political scandal. In his book *The Mind of Watergate* Rangell includes the transcript of a verbal investigation conducted by US Sen. Howard Baker as he questioned a suspect, Herbert L. Porter, a campaign aide to President Nixon:

Because the question-and-answer dialogue sets forth a basic issue worth pursuing, I'll repeat a segment of the account exactly as it transpired.

Baker: "Did you ever have any qualms about what you were doing? . . . I am probing into your state of mind, Mr. Porter."
Porter: [Uncomfortably] "I was not the one to stand up in a meeting and say that this should be stopped . . . . I mean . . . I kind of drifted along."
The questioning continued.

Q: "At any time did you ever think of saying, 'I do not think this is quite right, this is not quite the way it ought to be.' Did you ever think of that?"
A: "Yes, I did."
Q: "What did you do about it?"
A: "I did not do anything."
Q: "Why didn't you?"
A: [After evidence of much inner thought on his face]: "In all honesty, probably because of the fear of group pressure that would ensue, of not being a team player."[27]

Optimize magazine lists the ten universal characteristics of integrity that have helped me live a life above reproach and have served as healthy "character guardrails" for me over the years:

The Ten Universal Characteristics of Integrity

1. You know that little things count.
2. You find the white when others see gray.
3. You mess up, you 'fess up.
4. You create a culture of trust.
5. You keep your word.
6. You care about the greater good.
7. You're honest but modest.
8. You act like you're being watched.
9. You hire integrity.
10. You stay the course.[28]

II. Do Good, Be Great with Integrity Guardrails

Several years ago, I had the privilege of traveling to Mexico with my dear friend, Larry Meyers. Larry invited me to speak to a group of leaders at a conference center in the Mexican state of Chiapas, outside Mexico City.

Larry has trained thousands of leaders over the years and is highly respected in that area of Mexico for being a man who is doing good, to be Great.

At age sixty, Larry was told by a national organization that he was too old to represent the organization any longer. But Larry's inner qualities of tenacity and determination empowered him, and he refused to let those shortsighted words affect him. He went outside the United States to build an incredible organization that is truly beyond ordinary. I've had the honor of helping Larry build many churches and community centers over the years, and I'm always amazed every time I visit him by how impressive his work is.

On a recent visit, I brought along with me several leaders from the Central Florida area to come with me to see firsthand the work Larry and his team were doing. The most difficult part of the trip to Larry's campus isn't the plane trip, the lodging, the food, or the people. It is the van ride from the airport in Chinalou, where his organization is located.

This wasn't my first visit to see Larry's work, which is located high in a rugged, mountainous location. The first time I had come, right away as we climbed the treacherous, winding mountain road, I noticed it had no guardrails. In America we see guardrails on just about every road that needs one, but in Mexico, they are very rare—practically nonexistent. Then as he drove us high into the mountains, Larry very calmly told me about all the accidents that happened on that road every week. As he relayed the horrific stories, I was as calm as could be on the outside, but inside I was panicking! I tried to look straight ahead and keep my eyes from straying over the cliffs to the rocky bottom thousands of feet below. It was a ride I will never forget!

What had I done? I had brought friends from America and shared with them the same fear I had experienced on my first visit to Larry's work! Within minutes, the team of men with me were absolutely terrified—a few almost in tears (I won't name them here). Many were physically sick and several were traumatized. In fact, one friend told me he would never ever ride on that road again. He's still my friend—but no friend of that experience!

What affected us the most on that ride was the fact that there were no guardrails. Guardrails keep you on the road. Guardrails help you avoid catastrophic accidents. Guardrails warn you that danger is nearby. Guardrails add a sense of security to your journey and lower the fear factor.

In our journey to move from doing good to do good, be Great, we all need what I call "integrity guardrails." Integrity guardrails keep us on the right track. They help us avoid personal disasters and warn us of impending tragedy. Without these guardrails, we travel on very dangerous roads that can lead to tremendous trouble and hardship. Those who desire to lead beyond ordinary lives have learned the key of having these guardrails to help keep them safe and avoid deadly danger.

Most of the time we get off track and fall into trouble and hardship when we refuse to establish "character guardrails." We go down the road of life without morals and values that help us stay safe. When we wreck, we have no one else to blame but ourselves, really. I call this "self-sabotage." Many times, the most dangerous person in any of our lives is ourselves. If you desire to live beyond ordinary, one key you should learn and live by is the revelation that you are your worst enemy. Here are a few points to help you avoid the most dangerous part of you:

Ways to Avoid the Most Dangerous Part of You

If you want to avoid self-sabotage:

1. **Stay Accountable:** Surround yourself with at least three people you can tell anything to, anytime. Make sure they will be available to hold you accountable and away from danger.
2. **Stay Connected:** These days we are more "connected" than ever before, yet so isolated and disconnected. Don't hide behind social networking and think it is reality. Stay connected with one-on-one, face-to-face, eyeball-to-eyeball, real relationships.
3. **Stay Focused:** On the road of life, it is very easy to fall asleep and veer off into the ditch. Stay alert and focused, and make sure you

are aware at all times. Drifting one little degree off the middle of the road can lead to hardship and disaster.

4. **Stay Humble:** Everyone—and I mean everyone—can fail and fall; no one is exempt. Pride is the greatest reason that people wreck their lives, marriages, careers, and relationships. Choose daily to remain humble and contrite.

5. **Stay Approachable:** You should make sure that anyone you surround yourself with has access to you. They should be able to come to you directly and speak with you about issues or concerns they have with your character and integrity. Don't hide behind committees, staff members, or boards to shield yourself from being approachable.

6. **Stay Busy:** The old saying, "Idleness is the devil's workshop," is still as true today as it ever was. When you're idle, you're accessible to temptations that you would not have if you were active and busy. Leaders who desire to do good Great should be aware of this trap.

7. **Stay Open:** Don't become closed-minded regarding issues of character and integrity. Be open to insights, suggestions, or opinions from tasteful friends. Be open when people point out the hidden things you do not see about yourself.

8. **Stay Teachable:** I have seen so many gifted leaders who think they have arrived and no longer feel the need to receive correction, suggestions, or opinions. You are never too important not to hear advice that can help you avoid a crash.

9. **Stay Real:** Many times people who reach success lose reality. They think they have arrived and they change into a different person; they cease living in reality. Be honest with yourself and others when you are addressing your character and integrity.

10. **Stay Honest:** You can't lie to others and to yourself forever. That kind of living will eventually catch up with you. Be honest with yourself and others. Avoiding honesty will surely set you up for future tragedy and heartache.

Character Guardrails: Common Claims of Wrecked Lives
Over the years I have personally witnessed and talked with many people who did not live lives of character and integrity. For whatever reason, they chose not to put up guardrails for their journey. They veered off the cliff and destroyed their lives as well as the lives of many others. I think it's healthy to be reminded that as leaders, when we choose to live our lives without guardrails and wreck ourselves due to moral failure, we needlessly wreck the lives of countless innocent bystanders as well. Here are a few common traits of people I've seen or known who have failed to live in integrity:

1. Insist "The wreck happened suddenly, without warning!"
People who wreck their lives don't get an email that day saying, "Today you will wreck your life." Most of the time, the crash comes unannounced. Suddenly they say, "The wreck happened suddenly, without warning!"

2. Embrace the, "it will never happen to me," attitude.
Most times, people are in denial and don't think they will ever wreck. They believe they live above the natural laws of life.

3. Ignore warning signs.
Sometimes, by grace, people are given a warning signal that something is not right and they had better take notice. Much like the "check engine" light that comes on in our cars, we get little signals that something is off track. If you ignore the signs, there will be trouble ahead. Pay attention to the signs.

4. They didn't establish guardrails soon enough.
Character guardrails need to be established *before* you're out of control— when you're going over the cliff is not the time. Trust me; you don't have time to set up your guardrails when you are spinning all over the road, fighting for control, and heading for a certain wreck. *Now* is the time to

set the standards that will help you when an issue arises. Do it now; it's not too late.

5. They didn't realize how much damage they were capable of doing.
Character guardrails help you limit the ultimate damage. The damage from hitting a guardrail and being bounced back into the middle of the road is far less than damage from going over a cliff. When you hit a guardrail, it may hurt a little, but the impact warns you to get back in the lane. Without guardrails, damage is unlimited. Instead of staying on the road with minor damage, you can find yourself with a life that is "totaled."

As Coach John Wooden once said:

"There are no insignificant moral choices; your 'little' decisions invariably impact your life in a big way."[29]

Character Versus Reputation

I have always looked up to John Wooden as a role model and a hero. The "Wizard of Westwood," as he was called, led the UCLA Bruins basketball team to a never equaled ten NCAA national championships. Without question, Coach Wooden is the greatest college basketball coach in history, which is why Pat Williams wrote a book about his life, *How to Be Like Coach Wooden: Life Lessons from Basketball's Greatest Leader.* Shortly before that book was released, Pat asked Coach Wooden to reflect on "character"—what it is, where it comes from, and how one can maintain it.

"I first became aware of the importance of character in my grade school days," Coach Wooden said. "From the time I was very young, my father would say: 'Be more concerned with your character than with your reputation. Your character is what you really are. Your reputation is merely how you are perceived by others.' When I graduated from grade school, my father gave me a piece of paper on which he had written, 'Son, always try to live up to this.' Today I call his advice 'The Seven-Point Creed.'"

As he said this, Coach Wooden gave Pat a copy of The Seven-Point Creed:

1. Be true to yourself.
2. Make each day your masterpiece.
3. Help others.
4. Drink deeply from good books, especially the Bible.
5. Make friendship a fine art.
6. Build a shelter against a rainy day.
7. Pray for guidance and give thanks for your blessings every day.[30]

"I hope I shall possess firmness and virtue enough to maintain what I consider the most enviable of all titles, the character of an honest man."
(George Washington, First American President)

"My strength is as the strength of ten, because my heart is pure."
(Alfred Lord Tennyson, Nineteenth-Century English Poet)

Questions for you on ....
Chapter 7: Do Good, Be Great With Integrity Guardrails

1. When you read about Bill Gates, what are some of the do good be great qualities you see?

2. Pick out one of the quotes from Bill Gates and discuss why this particular quote inspires you.

3. What does character look like to you? Describe some of the characteristics of character in someone you know who is close to you.

4. What's the difference between image and integrity?

5. Integrity guardrails...what do they mean to you? Describe what guardrails you have in place to keep you safe.

6. Do you know someone who did not have integrity guardrails? What price did they pay for not having those safeguards in place?

Notes

Great Quotes from a Great Leader
Princess Diana

- *"Carry out a random act of kindness, with no expectation of reward, safe in the knowledge that one day someone might do the same for you."*
- *"Anywhere I see suffering that is where I want to be, doing what I can."*
- *"Nothing brings me more happiness than trying to help the most vulnerable people in society. It is a goal and an essential part of my life—a kind of destiny. Whoever is in distress can call on me. I will come running wherever they are."*
- *"I want to walk into a room, be it a hospital for the dying or a hospital for the sick children, and feel that I am needed. I want to do, not just to be."*
- *"Every one of us needs to show how much we care for each other and, in the process, care for ourselves."*
- *"You can't comfort the afflicted with afflicting the comfortable."*
- *"Hugs can do great amounts of good—especially for children."*
- *"I want my boys to have an understanding of people's emotions, their insecurities, people's distress, and their hopes and dreams."*

8

Do Good, Be Great by Staying True to Your True North

KEY 8: BEYOND ORDINARY PEOPLE STAY TRUE TO THEIR TRUE NORTH

PRINCESS DIANA—A Shining Star: Do Good, Be Great for Those Who Have No Voice

I n the early morning of August 31, 1997, Britain's Princess Diana died from injuries she suffered in a horrific, high-speed car crash on the streets of Paris. Diana and three others were trying to elude a cadre of paparazzi at about thirty minutes past midnight when their Mercedes sedan sped inside the narrow Pont de l'Alma underpass. A split-second later, driver Henri Paul lost control of the car, which slammed head-on into a concrete pillar at eighty-five miles an hour.

Diana's romantic companion, Dodi Fayed, along with Paul, died at the crash site a half mile from the Eiffel Tower. Only Diana's bodyguard, Trevor Rees-Jones, would survive. Mortally injured, Diana was moved to a local hospital, where doctors attempted emergency treatments on her until 4 a.m. Paris time, when she was officially declared dead. Her tragic death at age thirty-six robbed the world of one of the most iconic figures of the twentieth century. Diana, Princess of Wales had become known across the globe as the "people's princess"—a visibly shy young lady of British aristocracy who blossomed into one of the most glamorous and admired women on the planet. Her funeral in Westminster Abbey, London, a week later was broadcast live on television and aired worldwide by the BBC. Elton John's moving performance of his song "Candle in the Wind," written about Marilyn Monroe but offered to Diana, became an unforgettable tribute.

She had been born Lady Diana Spencer on July 1, 1961, in Norfolk, on the eastern coast of England. A gracefully beautiful girl with natural poise and elegance, Diana rapidly stole the camera's eye from Prince Charles—heir to the British throne and twelve years her senior—after he proposed to her when she was nineteen. They married in storybook fashion in 1981 at St. Paul's Cathedral, London, amid royal heraldry, pomp, and ceremony. William, their first son, was born in 1982, making Diana the mother of a king-to-be, and in 1984 the couple's second and last child, Harry, was born.

As Princess of Wales, Diana regularly appeared at hospitals, schools, and other facilities, undertaking as many as 397 public appearances one year. In 1989, she became president of Great Ormond Street Hospital for Children in London, and from 1984 to 1996, she was president of Barnardo's—a charity founded by Dr. Thomas Barnardo in 1866 to care for the city's vulnerable children and youth. As the patron of the British Deaf Association, she learned to sign.

Diana became especially interested in serious and deadly illnesses, including AIDS and leprosy. She devoted much time to humanitarian work, assisting alongside noteworthy individuals such as Mother Teresa, and her visits frequently took her to the bedsides of the terminally ill. She was also the patron of charities and organizations that dedicated to the homeless, drug addicts, young people, and the elderly.

"Carry out a random act of kindness with no expectation of reward," she exhorted, "safe in the knowledge that one day someone might do the same for you."

In 1995, while in Moscow to present medical equipment to a children's hospital, she received the international Leonardo Award, given to the most distinguished patrons and people in the arts, medicine, and sports. In 1997, receptions were held in London and New York at which several dresses and suits worn by the princess while on official engagements were sold, with the proceeds going to charity.

Whether she appeared at a homeless shelter or the home of a head of state, Diana was the headliner. Her name alone created a publicity draw that no celebrity or entertainer's name could match. Her presence at a premiere would draw upwards of $100,000 for whatever charity was involved. The press enjoyed pointing out that all of Britain—and especially the royal family—had never seen anything like her.

During the early 1990s, her once storybook marriage to Prince Charles unraveled. Their divorce was finalized in August 1996, with each one blaming the other's indiscretions for their matrimonial meltdown. Sensationalized news reports quickly followed, and when the media pitted them against each other in a duel for sympathetic public opinion, Diana always bested Charles—a fact that inevitably would shake the ground beneath the rest of the royal family. In particular, the tempestuous relationship between the queen and the princess was succulent fodder for tabloid and mainstream journalists alike.

To the very end, the camera adored Diana more than Charles. Tragically, it was the public's ravenous appetite for more glossy images of Diana that spurred the paparazzi into the deadly pursuit that ended her life. By then, Diana had been transformed from the shy debutante of English high society into the global icon who embodied not just elegance and sophistication, but a level of humanitarianism not seen among the modern monarchy of Great Britain.

Continuing her charitable efforts today is the Diana, Princess of Wales, Memorial Fund, which was established after her death. It supplies grants and supports initiatives to provide care for the sick in Africa, aid refugees, and halt the use of land mines.

Despite her lofty place in society, Diana made a life-changing connection with people outside her privileged sphere. As a result, she won the respect of millions of people for her efforts to do good, be Great. In 1999, *Time* magazine named her one of the 100 Most Important People of the 20th Century. In 2002, Diana numbered third on the BBC's poll of the 100 Greatest Britons, outranking the queen.

In 2007, to mark the tenth anniversary of the death of their mother, sons William and Harry honored her with a concert on what would have been her forty-sixth birthday, with proceeds going to charities the three of them supported. Though she was the mother of a future king, she would never be a queen. Knowing it after her divorce, she said she hoped instead to become "a queen in people's hearts." It was a goal she realized.

My "True North"

If there ever was a shining star that followed her True North, it was Princess Diana. She was an inspiration to millions of people, not only in England and Europe but worldwide too. Her compassion for the underdog made her beautiful both inside and out. I'm reminded of the touching moment at her funeral when Elton John sang his song, *"Candle in the Wind,"* with the lyrics, "Your candle burned out long before your legend ever did," which was both poetic and prophetic.

One attribute that has intrigued me about Princess Diana was her innate ability to stay in tune with her source of personal destiny and purpose. Despite all the controversy and misunderstandings about her marriage and her royal status, she stayed with what I call her True North.

Whenever I get the chance, I absolutely love sitting in my backyard with my wife, Tammi, and our children, after a long day at the office. I am blessed to have a home that truly is my small castle. After a family meal, it's so relaxing to sit by our pool and unwind, talk, and laugh. We've lived in our house for fifteen years, and it wasn't until a few years ago that I noticed as we sat in our lawn chairs (which faced due east), that we could see a bright star, which is actually the planet Venus. Although it is not positioned specifically north, it conveys for me a sense of peace, tranquility, and focus. I can't really explain it, but when I look up and see that star, it gives me a feeling of comfort and stability.

As I write this chapter, I am approximately 2,500 miles away from my home, in Silmena, Malawi, at a conference center called The Red Zebra Inn. It's a beautiful campus on the shores of Lake Malawi, one of the largest lakes in the world. It's been over two weeks now that I've been away from my Central Florida home. Although I am not with my family or my wife, I can look up and immediately locate that bright star to the east! I'm filled with that same sense of tranquility and balance. There's just something very special about discovering your True North—finding the real you and the real purpose for which you were created and living with the sense of direction, focus, and stability.

The Rodriguez Family: Trying to Stay on Course

The Rodriguez family was living the American dream: great marriage, fun-filled home, good-paying jobs, and healthy children. Their world came crashing down when they were informed that their youngest son, Jose, had a life-threatening illness. The doctors in their hometown of Columbus, Ohio, didn't have many options for them—other than to tell them to get to Orlando and see if Arnold Palmer Hospital could possibly help them. So, they did what any other loving parent would do under that circumstance: They packed up their belongings and headed to Florida for a life-altering adventure that would hopefully heal their son and give them a new outlook on life.

They left their home, jobs, family, and friends, in order to help Jose receive the care he needed to survive. Distant relatives offered them a place to stay when they arrived in Orlando, but after a few days, it proved to be too much to handle for both families, and the offer was retracted. Suddenly, they found themselves homeless and out of options. The hospital provided wonderful care and attention for Jose, but couldn't offer much help in the way of long-term housing or employment leads for mom and dad.

The hospital social worker met with Jose's mom, Jenny, one day to help with their crisis. With a long list of Central Florida nonprofits and charities in her folder that possibly would be able to offer the Rodriguez family some relief, the social worker led Jenny to a window that faced south and pointed in the direction of our Community Food and Outreach Center (CFOC). Our campus is just a few miles south of the hospital. Pointing out the window, she told Jenny: "Here's a list of places from which you might be able to get help, but if I were you, I would go to that place on Michigan Street. Go there and you'll get help."

After a few weeks of phone calls, meetings, and clinical assessments, the caring staff at CFOC was able to secure the Rodriguez family long-term housing, jobs for both Markus and Jenny, and placement of their children in public schools. A local car dealer donated an automobile to them. Most important, Jose was given a new lease on life.

Jenny never gave up! Her thoughts remained strong and hopeful even in her darkest moments. She always believed and thought that things would turn around for her and her family. Sickness was a strong foe, but Jenny's ability to think positively empowered her to make it through the family's difficult situation.

Jenny realized that there were many forces trying to get her and her family off course. Her son's sickness caused the family to understandably veer off course and stray from her True North, which was to live a life of service to others. Jenny had always dreamed of being a nurse and helping people, but her dream was sidetracked and delayed by difficult circumstances.

What Is Your True North?

Do you know what your life and your leadership are all about, and when you are being true to yourself? True North is the internal compass that guides you successfully through life. It represents who you are as a human being at your deepest level. It is your orienting point—your fixed point in a spinning world—that helps you stay on track as a leader. Your True North is based on what is most important to you, your most cherished values, your passions and motivations, the sources of satisfaction in your life.

Just as a compass points toward a magnetic pole, your True North pulls you toward the purpose of your leadership. When you follow your internal compass, your leadership will be authentic, and people will naturally want to associate with you. Although others may guide or influence you, your truth is derived from your life story, and only you can determine what it should be.[31]

Clock or Compass?

"Time waits for no man." You've probably heard that saying. And it's true; time marches on, and it's up to us to keep up with it. We need to be conscious of the clock, or we'll never make any progress toward our goals. But I believe there's more to success than reaching goals. True success comes from significance: doing things that matter . . . things that last after we're gone.

How do we know if what we're doing really makes a difference? We can't just look at the clock. We need to be conscious of our compass.

For many people, the first half of life is consumed by the clock. As young adults, we're very conscious of time. We're impatient, eager to "get started" with life. Later, as we start achieving goals, we're still watching the clock: We want to measure how much we're accomplishing. Usually sometime in our forties, most of us become aware of the compass. We begin to wonder why we're doing what we're doing. We question the value of what we've achieved. We examine whether we're fulfilled. And then we worry that we're not making a difference in this world.

Ideally, as we get older, we start trying to achieve balance between the clock and the compass. We try to be conscious of both, which makes us more strategic. We ask, *What can I do that will make the most difference in the time that I have?* We start talking about leaving a legacy.

Ultimately, I believe that no matter what age we are, we all need to seek a balance between the clock and the compass. In other words, we need to integrate a daily focus with a long-term sense of direction. This gives us a better perspective.

The Clock: The clock is always ticking in this life. Time passes, and we either take advantage of opportunities, or we miss them. So it's important to keep the clock in mind. But it's not the only thing, if you want to live a life of significance.

The Compass: The compass is what we use to steer life. It remains constant, and we're wise when we align ourselves with the direction we know we should be going. But just lining up with the compass doesn't get us anywhere if we don't start moving.

The clock equals daily things: *what* we are doing. The compass equals destiny things: *where* we are going. The clock deals with appointments and activities. The compass points toward vision, values, and mission. Together, the clock and the compass provide us with both motivation and direction. Finding a balance between them means that we're able to compound our efforts and add the most value we can to our world.

So the next time you plan your day, week, or year, be conscious of both the clock and the compass, and see how far it takes you.[32]
(John Maxwell)

Enemies of Your True North
7 *Dream Killers That Steal Your True North*

1. **Foes**—Many foes will try to keep you off track and distracted. Make sure you stay on course and focused.
   "A thief is only there to steal and kill and destroy. I came so they (you) can have real and eternal life, more and better life than they (you) ever dreamed of" (John 10:10, The Message Bible, parentheses added).
2. **Family**—Many times, those closest to you are the ones who will try to keep you from discovering your destiny. Don't let family keep you from do good, be Great.
   "When he told his father as well as his brothers, his father rebuked him" (Genesis 37:10, NIV).
   "No prophet is accepted in his hometown" (Luke 4:24, NIV).
3. **Friends**—Show me who you spend the most time with, and I will show you what you will believe.
   "Walk with the wise and become wise, for a companion of fools suffers harm" (Proverbs 13:20, NIV). "Do not be deceived: 'Bad company ruins good morals'" (1 Corinthians 15:33).
   "Keep away from people who try to belittle your ambitions. Small people always do that, but the really great make you feel that you, too, can become great. When you are seeking to bring big plans to fruition, it is important with whom you regularly associate. Hang out with

friends who are like-minded and who are also designing purpose-filled lives. Similarly, be that kind of a friend for your friends." (Mark Twain)

4. **Fears**—Fears will paralyze and immobilize you. Don't let fears keep you from living the beyond ordinary life.

   "So do not fear, for I am with you; do not be dismayed, for I am your God. I will strengthen you and help you; I will uphold you with my righteous right hand" (Isaiah 41:10, NIV).

   "We gain strength, and courage, and confidence by each experience in which we really stop to look fear in the face . . . we must do that which we think we cannot."
   (Eleanor Roosevelt)

   To fight fear . . . Believe
   To increase fear . . . Wait
   To enlarge fear . . . Think
   To reduce fear . . . Pray
   To eliminate fear . . . Act

5. **Failure**—Past failure is no clear indication of future failure. Most people who have tasted success have also faced many trials and mistakes. Make sure you learn from your failures and move on.

   "For though the righteous fall seven times, they rise again" *(Proverbs 24:16, NIV).*

   "Far better is it to dare mighty things, to win glorious triumphs, even though checkered by failure . . . than to rank with those poor spirits who neither enjoy nor suffer much, because they live in a gray twilight that knows not victory nor defeat."
   (Theodore Roosevelt)

   "Many of life's failures are people who did not realize how close they were to success when they gave up."   (Thomas A. Edison)

6. **Fatigue**—Many people are only a day, week, or month from achieving their dreams, but they give up too easily because they are tired. The race is not for the swift, but for those who can endure.

In the last days, God says, I will pour out my Spirit on all people. Your sons and daughters will prophesy, your young men will see visions, your old men will dream dreams'" (Acts 2:17, NIV).
"You are never too old to dream a new dream."
(C. S. Lewis)
"Our fatigue is often caused not by work, but by worry, frustration, and resentment.
(Dale Carnegie)

7. **Frustration**—Those who desire to do good, and be Great learn the key to success is overcoming frustration. As you conquer frustration, you will see your dreams become a reality.
    "Let us not become weary in doing good, for at the proper time we will reap a harvest if we do not give up" (Galatians 6:9, NIV).
    "Frustration, although quite painful at times, is a very positive and essential part of success."
    (Bo Bennett)

How to Unlock Your True North

1. Discover Your Purpose

In Kevin McCarthy's great book, *On Purpose*, he clearly and effectively defines and explains how we unlock our purpose, vision, mission, and values:

Purpose is being
Vision is seeing
Missions are doing
Values are choosing
To be on purpose, you begin with your being (purpose), it sparks your seeing (vision), which then puts into action your doing (mission). The linkage of purpose, vision, and mission is governed by your choosing (values). When your being and seeing and doing and choosing are all aligned and integrated, then you are on your purpose, or being on purpose.[34]

Spencer Johnson from *The One Minute Salesperson* said it best:

A purpose is ongoing and gives meaning to our lives. When people have a purpose in life, they enjoy everything they do. People go on chasing goals to prove something that doesn't have to be proved, that they are already worthwhile. The fastest way to achieve goals, the successful salesperson said, "is to stay on purpose." [35]

Norman Vincent Peale motivates us to seek out our purpose so we can serve others:

We are here to be excited from youth to old age, to have an insatiable curiosity about the world. We are also here to help others by practicing a friendly attitude, and every person is born for a purpose. Everyone has a God-given potential, in essence, built into them, and if we are to live life to its fullest, we must realize that potential. [36]

2. Face and Conquer Your Fears
9 Ways to Defeat Your Fear

In a speech in 1933, President Franklin Roosevelt, addressing our nation that was mired in the Great Depression and on the verge of a world war, famously stated, "The only thing we have to fear is fear itself." During the first century AD, Epicetetus said, "It is not death or pain that is to be dreaded, but the fear of pain or death." And in the 1600s, Francis Bacon remarked that, "Nothing is terrible except fear itself."

Fear is universal. It crosses all boundaries of race, culture, religion, and generation. We all feel fear. So why do some people appear to be fearless, doing battle with enemies that others cower before? Because they recognize that the greatest enemy they face is the fear itself. Fear is a powerful force and it has the power to motivate you or immobilize you.

So how should we deal with fear? Avoiding it never really makes it go away; we either become paralyzed or defeated.

The only way to deal with fear is to face it and overcome it. Dale Carnegie explained it this way: "Inaction breeds doubt and fear. Action breeds confidence and courage. If you want to conquer fear, do not sit home and think about it. Go out and get busy."

Here are the 9 actions you can take to face and overcome fear:

1. Discover the source of fear

The fact is that most fear is not based on fact. Much of what we fear is based on a feeling. According to an old saying, "Fear and worry are interest paid in advance on something you may never own." And Aristotle explained, "Fear is pain arising from anticipation of evil." The real foundation of fear is based on feeling and is not reality.

When you acknowledge that the majority of fear is unfounded, you can begin to release yourself from its power. US Army General George Patton understood this. He said, "I learned very early in life not to take counsel of my fears." Businessman Allen Neuharth saw his worst fears come true, only to realize that they weren't as big as he had imagined: "I quit being afraid when my first venture failed and the sky didn't fall down."

2. 'Fess up to your fears

One of our biggest misconceptions is that courage equals a lack of fear. Actually, the opposite is true. Mark Twain explained, "Courage is resistance to fear, mastery of fear—not absence of fear." By admitting our fear, we can then challenge its accuracy.

That's how General Patton dealt with it: "The time to take counsel of your fears is before you make an important battle decision," he said. "That's the time to listen to every fear you can imagine! When you have collected all the facts and fears and made your decision, turn off all of your fears and go ahead!"

3. Acknowledge the frailty and brevity of life

Sometimes our greatest fears are founded on reality. For example, we are all going to die sometime. There's no denying that. Likewise, life will often be hard and painful. Those things are completely out of our control. By accepting their reality, we can then focus on the things we actually can control.

I love what Gertrude Stein wrote about fear: *"Considering how dangerous everything is, nothing is really frightening."*

4. Realize that fear is the price of progress
"As long as I continue to push out into the world," said Susan Jeffers, "as long as I continue to stretch my capabilities, as long as I continue to take risks in making my dreams come true, I am going to experience fear."

To do anything of value, we have to take risks. And with risk comes fear. If we accept it as the price of progress, then we can take appropriate risks that yield great reward.

5. Choose to face fear head on
Sometimes the best way to fight fear is to focus on our reason for confronting it. Is our goal bigger than the fear? The firefighter runs into the burning building not because he's fearless, but because he has a calling that is more important than the fear. Choose today not to run from your fears but to hit them head on.

6. Concentrate on what you can control
We cannot control the length of our lives; we can't control many of the circumstances we face. Accepting those facts allows us to focus on what we can control. Like basketball coach John Wooden said, "Do not let what you cannot do interfere with what you can do."

As a leader, I often have to deal with the wrong attitudes and actions of the people who follow me. So a long time ago, I decided that:

> *I can control my attitude, but not others' actions.*
> *I can control my calendar, but not others' circumstances.*
> *What's most important is not what happens to me, but what happens in me.*

7. *Focus on today*

Fear tries to make us look at all our problems at once: those from yesterday, today, and tomorrow. To be courageous, you have to focus only on today. Why? Because it's the only thing you have any control over.

I love what a wise man once said about an ocean liner: "If an ocean liner could think and feel, it would never leave its dock; it would be afraid of the thousands of huge waves it would encounter. It would fear all of its dangers at once, even though it had to meet them only one wave at a time."

By focusing only on what's right in front of us, we can manage tremendous risk because we know we'll only have to deal with it one wave at a time.

8. *Put some wins under your belt*

Just like fear tends to breed more fear, courage leads to more courage. According to Eleanor Roosevelt, wife of President Franklin Roosevelt: "You gain strength, courage, and confidence by every experience in which you really stop to look fear in the face. You are able to say to yourself: 'I lived through this horror. I can take the next thing that comes along.' You must do the thing you think you cannot do." The more we face our fears, the more capable we begin to feel, and the more fears we are willing to face.

9. *Now is the time for action*

Often, all it takes to conquer a fear is to change our focus and try some of the above suggestions. As we realize what's true and focus on what we can control, the fear naturally fades and weakens. But there are other times when no amount of thinking can overcome the fear. In fact, the more we think in those situations, the more fearful we become. At those times, the only solution is action.

As W. Clement Stone said, "When thinking won't cure fear, action will."

It is the wise person who accepts fear as a very real part of life and that it must be faced and overcome with courage. By taking action in the face of fear, he or she achieves results and becomes more courageous.

Another US president, Harry S. Truman, said it this way: "The worst danger we face is the danger of being paralyzed by doubts and fears. This danger is brought on by those who abandon faith and sneer at hope. It is brought on by those who spread cynicism and distrust and try to blind us to our great chance to do good for all mankind."

The man who succeeds above his fellows is the one who early in life clearly discerns his object, and towards that object habitually directs his powers.
Even genius itself is but fine observation strengthened by fixity of purpose.
Every man who observes vigilantly and resolves steadfastly grows unconsciously into genius.
(Edward George Bulwer-Lytton, 1803-1873, English novelist)

3. Stay Your Course

Your True North star, or in my case, my true east star, will assist you to stay on course. At times, when you are tempted to get off course, your undeniable purpose and courage to face fear will keep you to do good, be Great and live beyond ordinary.

Pits to Avoid to Stay on Course

"The mass of men lead lives of quiet desperation." (Henry David Thoreau, 1817-1862)
The man without a purpose is
like a ship without a rudder—
waif, a nothing, a no man.
Have a purpose in life, and, having it,
throw such strength of mind
and muscle into your work
as God has given you."
(Thomas Carlyle, 1795-1881)

1. Pit of Distraction

There will be many distractions that will try to pull at you and get you off course. Do not be distracted and stray from your true calling and purpose.

2. The Pit of Discouragement
When you are following your God-given purpose and destiny, there will be opportunities for you to get discouraged and lose your focus because of discouragement. Choose to move beyond this pit to stay on track.

3. The Pit of Defeat
Just because you have failed in your past does not make you a failure. John Maxwell encourages us to "fall forward" and not allow the pit of defeat to keep us from discovery or destiny.

4. The Pit of Delay
Delay is not denial! Just because you are not fully seeing things fall into place does not mean it won't happen. Be patient and stay focused as you are in a time of delay.

> *Until you value yourself,*
> *you will not value your time.*
> *Until you value your time,*
> *you will not do anything with it.*
> (M. Scott Peck, MD, *1936-2005, The Road Less Traveled*)

> *I am afraid to show you who I really am,*
> *because if I show you who I really am,*
> *you might not like it—and that's all I got.*
> (Sabrina Ward Harrison, artist and author)

> *Each of us possesses a moral GPS, a compass or conscience programmed by parents, teachers, coaches, grandparents, clergy, friends, and peers. The compass is an integral part of our being. It continues to differentiate between proper and improper behavior until the day we die.*[36]
> (Jim Huntsman)

From Goodness to Greatness

Phillips Brooks, a nineteenth-century clergyman, wrote in *Purpose and Use of Comfort*, "Greatness after all, in spite of its name, appears to be not so much a certain size as a certain quality in human lives. It may be present in lives whose range is very small."[37]

Questions for you on ....
Chapter 8: Do Good, Be Great by Staying True to Your
True North

1. When you read about Princess Diana, what are some of the do good be great qualities you see?

2. Pick out one of the quotes from Princess Diana and discuss why this particular quote inspires you.

3. Describe your true north and how does it guide you towards greatness?

4. There are 7 dream killers that steal your true north. List out the killers that most affect you.

5. In regard to our true north, what is the difference between a clock and a compass?

6. The only thing we have to fear is fear itself. What is your greatest fear that you are facing today and how can you conquer this fear?

Notes

Great Quotes from a Great Leader
Martin Luther King

- *"We must accept finite disappointment, but never lose infinite hope."*
- *"True compassion is more than flinging a coin to a beggar; it comes to see that an edifice which produces beggars needs restructuring."*
- *"Life's most persistent and urgent question is: What are you doing for others?"*
- *"Those who are not looking for happiness are the most likely to find it, because those who are searching forget that the surest way to be happy is to seek happiness for others."*
- *"We must live together as brothers or perish together as fools."*
- *"The first question which the priest and the Levite asked was: 'If I stop to help this man, what will happen to me?' But . . . the good Samaritan reversed the question: 'If I do not stop to help this man, what will happen to him?'"*
- *"No work is insignificant. All labor that uplifts humanity has dignity and importance and should be undertaken with painstaking excellence."*
- *"Without love, there is no reason to know anyone, for love will in the end connect us to our neighbors, our children, and our hearts."*
- *"The difference between a dreamer and a visionary is that a dreamer has his eyes closed and a visionary has his eyes open."*
- *"Christ furnished the spirit and motivation while Gandhi furnished the method."*
- *"Faith is taking the first step even when you don't see the whole staircase."*

9

Do Good, Be Great When Life Sends a Storm

KEY 9: BEYOND ORDINARY PEOPLE DANCE IN THE RAIN WHEN LIFE SENDS A STORM

DR. MARTIN LUTHER KING JR.—Do Good, Be Great for Those Struggling in Bondage

On December 1, 1955, a black woman named Rosa Parks refused to give up her seat to a white man on a crowded bus in Montgomery, Alabama. Her courageous act of peaceful resistance to racial segregation sparked a national civil rights movement unlike anything America had seen. Leading the movement from day one was a young, unknown, but powerful prophetic voice—Martin Luther King Jr.—whose vision for do good, be Great was ahead of its time. In thirteen short years, he would rise from obscurity to become the greatest social justice advocate in US history.

Martin was still a new face amid Montgomery's black community at the time that Parks stayed in her seat to make a stand against segregationist law. Like his father and grandfather before him, Martin was a preacher. Only a year before had he become pastor of the local congregation at Dexter Avenue Baptist Church. Still in his mid-twenties, he was just starting his clerical career.

Yet the youthful face in the pulpit at Dexter Avenue Baptist belied the depth of the soul behind it. Excellent at academics, Martin had graduated at age fifteen from his segregated public school in Atlanta, Georgia—the city where he was born "Michael" on January 15, 1929, and later renamed Martin Jr. after his father. He earned his bachelor's degree from Atlanta's respected Morehouse College, then undertook postgraduate studies at Crozer Seminary in Pennsylvania before being awarded a doctorate from Boston University.

During Martin's first year in Montgomery, the black elders of the city's clerical community had taken note of the young preacher, recognizing him to be a gifted orator. They quickly recruited him to serve as spokesman for the newly formed Montgomery Bus Boycott, which had been organized in the wake of Parks' action and formed in order to force integration of the city's bus lines.

On December 5, blacks from across Montgomery started gathering four hours early for a mass meeting in Holt Street Baptist Church scheduled at 7 p.m. King's address to them would be his first as a civil rights leader.

"I want to tell you this evening that it is not enough for us to talk about love," he told the packed church. "Love is one of the pivotal points of the Christian faith. There is another side called justice . . . . Justice is love correcting that which revolts against love."

His speech stirred the crowd of approximately 1,000, and they stood and cheered when asked to support a resolution to boycott. The Montgomery Bus Boycott had begun and it lasted 381 days. Arrests ensued, and King's parsonage and another leader's home were bombed. But the nonviolent boycott rocked the legal foundations of the country. It led to a decisive victory in the US Supreme Court on November 13, 1956—a unanimous, one sentence judgment—ruling that racial segregation in transportation was unconstitutional.

Martin, however, had not quickly consented to his elders' request to be the boycott's spokesman. Perhaps he understood that his own life and those of his family would never be the same if he stepped into the pulpit and denounced racial inequality before the national media.

Whatever his reason for hesitating, when he accepted their request, it was as if in choosing he was being chosen. As if Providence had selected him—not as a mere spokesman, but as a prophet to his generation. Starting on that night at Holt Street Baptist, he would revolutionize not only the concept of, but also the application of justice in America, pinning it to civil rights while pricking the national conscience with a prophetic cry to banish racial segregation from the land.

In 1957, King was elected president of the Southern Christian Leadership Conference, a body formed to provide governance for the fast growing civil rights movement. In 1963, he led a coalition of civil rights groups in a nonviolent campaign targeting Birmingham, Alabama—described as the "most segregated city in America." Television images of young blacks being assaulted with dogs and water hoses vividly captured the subsequent brutality of the city's police. National outrage resulted, leading to a push for unprecedented civil rights legislation.

The Birmingham events culminated in the March on Washington for Jobs and Freedom on August 28, 1963. More than 200,000 people assembled at the Lincoln Memorial when King delivered his acclaimed "I Have a Dream" speech, predicting a time in America when there would be freedom and equality for all races.

In 1964, at age thirty-five, King became the youngest person at the time to win the Nobel Peace Prize. Often quoted from his acceptance speech in Oslo, Norway, is the phrase: "Right temporarily defeated is stronger than evil triumphant."

Also in 1964, due in part to the march on Washington, Congress passed the landmark Civil Rights Act, making it illegal to discriminate against blacks or other minorities in hiring, public accommodations, education, or transportation—each an area that was highly segregated.

The next year, Congress went on to pass the Voting Rights Act, which eliminated remaining barriers to voting for African-Americans. It resulted directly from the March for Voting Rights between Selma, Alabama, and Montgomery, Alabama, which King led.

King's short span of nonviolent civil rights leadership ended abruptly and tragically on April 4, 1968, when he was assassinated at the Lorraine

Motel in Memphis, Tennessee. He had achieved more genuine progress toward racial equality in America in thirteen years than had been created in the previous 350 years.

"Human progress is neither automatic nor inevitable," he said. "Every step toward the goal of justice requires . . . the tireless exertions and passionate concern of dedicated individuals."

Many others in King's day advocated for freedom "by any means necessary," including violence. For the most part, they are now forgotten. By contrast, King is regarded today as one of the greatest apostles of nonviolent change in world history.

His power to do good, be Great lay in the spoken word and in acts of peaceful civil resistance, much like that of Rosa Parks. Through them he was able to both uphold his convictions and demonstrate to the world that people everywhere, no matter their color or creed, are equal in worth.

■ ■ ■

I was recently on an international flight to speak to a group of pastors and leaders. The flight was more than sixteen hours, so after trying to sleep in a hundred different positions (at six feet four inches tall, it is problematic), I decided to try the media option and see if watching a movie would either put me to sleep or awaken me to endure the last few hours of the trip. When the selection time came to choose a film, the only movie that piqued my interest was *Selma*, based on the life of Martin Luther King Jr. and the march from Selma to Montgomery. The film both inspired me and energized me—so much so that I no longer desired sleep; I was moved to live beyond ordinary and do my best to do good, and be Great.

After I got home, I printed a copy of Dr. King's speech at the conclusion of the Montgomery march.

"We've come a long way since that travesty of justice was perpetrated upon the American mind. James Weldon Johnson put it eloquently. He said: 'We have come over a way that with tears hath been watered. (*Yes, sir*)We have come treading our paths through the blood of the slaughtered. (*Yes, sir*)Out of the gloomy past, (*Yes, sir*)Till now we stand at last where the white gleam of our bright star is cast.' (*Speak, sir*)

"Today I want to tell the city of Selma, (*Tell them, Doctor*) today I want to say to the state of Alabama, (*Yes, sir*) today I want to say to the people of America and the nations of the world, that we are not about to turn around. (*Yes, sir*) We are on the move now. (*Yes, sir*)

Yes, we are on the move and no wave of racism can stop us. (*Yes, sir*) We are on the move now. The burning of our churches will not deter us. (*Yes, sir*) The bombing of our homes will not dissuade us. (*Yes, sir*) We are on the move now. (*Yes, sir*) The beating and killing of our clergymen and young people will not divert us. We are on the move now. (*Yes, sir*) The wanton release of their known murderers would not discourage us. We are on the move now. (*Yes, sir*) Like an idea whose time has come, (*Yes, sir*) not even the marching of mighty armies can halt us. (*Yes, sir*) We are moving to the land of freedom." (*Yes, sir*)[38]

Dr. King walked, faced, and lived victories in the face of storms. He didn't avoid storms. He didn't run from them. He didn't pawn them off on others to face them. He faced them head-on and lived a beyond ordinary life. I trust his life and story won't lull you to sleep, but like they did for me, will energize you to keep facing and fighting the storms so you can see the rainbow at the end of the storm.

Facing the Storms of Life

In 1985, I confronted my very first storm with my new bride, Tammi, in Edmond, Oklahoma. We were enjoying a quiet, peaceful night when suddenly the weatherman broke into our TV show with a look of fear and a voice warning of danger, and alerted viewers in Oklahoma City, but specifically Edmond, to watch out for a tornado that had been sighted. Since we were rookies to the area, we had no idea how dangerous this situation had become. Naively, I went out to our backyard and, in a matter of seconds, I was no longer looking at a blip on the TV AccuWeather radar; I was face to face with a deadly tornado. I knew instantly that this was not good and we took cover—we literally feared for our lives.

After what seemed like an eternity, we left our pantry closet and were confronted with a citywide tragedy. Our entire neighborhood, beginning only a few houses away, had been completely destroyed. When I say "completely" destroyed, I mean entire houses leveled. Forty to fifty homes were simply gone. A couple more houses were torn down to their foundation. This was truly a major disaster for our small city of Edmond.

This was the first national disaster we would face as a young couple, but it wouldn't be our last. Storms come upon all of us from time to time, and the lessons I learned from this storm would help me weather the "storms of life" in the years to come.

People who desire to do good, and be Great will undoubtedly face storms. Dr. King was a leader who faced storms daily, yet amid the storms, he was able to find a refuge and develop a strength that would give him the courage to face the wind, rain, and storms that serve to make us better, not bitter. Do good, be Great people learn that when life sends a storm, you must dance in the rain and weather the winds. Then you will learn valuable lessons that will make you a better person.

In the next section, I will share the stories of three people I know who went through terrible storms of life, as well as a disastrous storm in my life. By looking at these stories, you will learn keys for surviving and thriving in the midst of life's storms. Armed with these keys, hopefully you, like Dr. King, will come out on the other end stronger and better, and dance in the rain when life sends a storm.

When the Storms of Life Hit You

I got a call from a friend one day, and expected it to simply be a casual call. This friend, Jordan, had been a donor to our ministry for a few years. His company had also been a corporate sponsor. Life was good for this family (and many others like them) in Central Florida; a nice-paying corporate job, nice house in the suburbs, a boat, a few kids in private school. I would see Jordan's family at school events; our children would hang out, spend the night, and play basketball together. From the outside, it appeared that life was good for Jordan and his family, but he had no idea what was about to hit him and hundreds of thousands of families in Florida. The worst economic storm in forty-two years was about to hit our local economy—and the world's economy—very hard. And due to our tourism-based economy, we were in for a very long storm indeed.

I hadn't realized how bad it would get until Jordan called one day and asked if he could volunteer, which I thought was a nice gesture. It wasn't until the end of that day, when I saw Jordan and talked with him, that I found out how tough that season had been for him.

Standing Strong in the Middle of a Storm

Jordan wasn't the only one. Between 2008 and 2010, I saw many families turn from generous donors to humbled clients. Brian, a donor just like Jordan, also exemplified the crushing blow our region faced.

Brian was a generous donor in 2007. He and his family had donated over $50,000 to our mission. These were not corporate gifts; they were gifts from their personal checking account. I had been privileged to speak at their church many times over the years, and they had heard about our food assistance program, the medical clinic, and so many other programs that they wanted to come and see. Once again, that "come and see" principle I learned from Mother Teresa's life and legacy. In fact, if you were to come to my office in Orlando, you would find her book, *Come and See*, on the coffee table that adorns my office.

When Mother Teresa would meet people, and they would speak with her and inquire about her ministry, she would simply say, "Come and see." I think some nonprofits and charities would rather not have friends and donors show up because not much is happening during the week. Many times, organizations hide behind glossy brochures and cute videos, but other than that, not much goes on day to day. I love giving people tours and letting them see firsthand what is taking place on our campus at 150

West Michigan Street. The over 525 hurting families in need that walk on our campus every day are met by friendly, smiling volunteers, passionate board members, and loyal staff. I say, "Come and see," every day, and give this invitation freely to anyone willing to take the time to see, feel, and touch our mission.

Brian was no exception. He and his family came and saw and gave. I was always very grateful and humbled by how God touched their hearts in such a big way to give so generously. But Brian had been hit by the financial storm just as Jordan had. I remember well the call from Brian when he let me know that he would be unable to donate to our ministry anymore because his business had been severely affected. In addition to his personal struggles, he was also taking care of his father whose home had been foreclosed on. I totally understood his dilemma and prayed with him and wished him the very best; I assured him he had our prayers and support, and I continue to be very grateful to this day for his support and kindness.

Storms of Life

Jordan was in the same boat as Brian. No one could fully understand the magnitude of this storm, but we were starting to see the debris. Real estate professionals, schoolteachers, government workers, police officers and firefighters; the storm took many casualties and it would take years for many to fully recover, though some have yet to do so.

Jordan finally got up enough nerve to stop by my office at the end of his volunteer service to tell me firsthand why he was volunteering that day. He shut the door behind him as he sat down in shame and disbelief at his circumstances. "Scott," he humbly said, "I've come to volunteer today because I need food for my family. I couldn't just take food from you today; I had to volunteer to make myself feel a bit better. But the reality is, I lost my job, my house is in jeopardy, and I've hit rock bottom in just the last few months. I need some help."

We gave Jordan and his family food that day.

Lessons I've Learned from the Storms I've Survived

1. Storms visit everyone

If you're trying to walk through life with the goal of never failing while dealing with storms, you are misled and misguided. It's not really a matter of if but when you will be faced with a storm. How will you react? Those who desire to do good, be Great will face storms. People who want to live beyond ordinary will have storms hit their lives, their marriages, their families, their children, and their business. Don't try to avoid the storms when they come. Face them head on and learn that no matter how fierce the storm, you can always dance in the rain.

In his book, *When Bad Things Happen to Good People*, Rabbi Harold Kushner writes: *"There is only one question which really matters: Why do bad things happen to good people? All other theological conversation is intellectually diverting . . . . Virtually every meaningful conversation I have ever had with people on the subject of God and religion has either started with this question, or gotten around to it before long."*[39]

2. Storms shouldn't be blamed

When a storm visits your life, marriage, children, or business, try not to use much energy trying to blame the storm. You need all the energy you can muster up. You can't afford to waste your energy on blaming the storm and asking, "Why me?" The storm should not be your focus; your attitude and demeanor, and how to properly respond to the storm you are facing must be.

3. Storms will either make you bitter or better

Storms have a way of revealing either the best or the worst in us. It's either going to make you better or bitter. I've seen the same storm have totally opposite results on two different people. Some collapse under the pressure. Some climb. Some mope. Some dance in the rain. Determine that you will be the one who comes out better after the storm passes.

Howard Schultz, CEO of Starbucks, once had a searing meeting with an investor who told him: "If you don't go along with my deal, you'll never work in this town again. You'll never raise another dollar. You'll be dog meat." On leaving the meeting, Schultz was overcome with tears. For two frenzied weeks, he prepared an alternative plan that met his $3.8 million financing goal and staved off the alternate investor. He writes:

> *If I had agreed to the terms the investor demanded, he would have taken away my dream. He could have fired me at whim and dictated the atmosphere and values of Starbucks. The passion, commitment, and dedication would have all disappeared.*[40]

4. Storms reveal the real you

Everyone seems happy and to be living a successful life when there are no rain clouds and storms on the horizon. When money is in the bank, the children are good, and business is booming, anyone can dance! And this says nothing about you—the real you. The real you is not revealed in good times. The real you is unveiled when the storms of life invade your marriage, business, or body. This is when the real you comes out. Anger, bitterness, depression, and pity are exposed when the storms come in. This is the real you, and the storm may be helping you by exposing these areas in your heart.

Losing a Loved One

When you meet Marilyn Carlson Nelson for the first time, you are struck by her warmth, her zest for life, and her optimism that by inspiring people to step up and lead, any problem can be solved. Yet this CEO of Carlson Companies has a far more complex story. As if it were yesterday, she can vividly recall the morning her husband and she heard that their beautiful nineteen-year-old daughter, Juliet, had been killed in an automobile accident.

That's the most profound test we've ever had, a test of our faith and our personal relationship. I lost my faith at the time and felt angry with God. But God didn't abandon me and didn't let me go. I discovered how valuable every day is and how valuable each person is. I decided to make whatever time I had left meaningful so that the time that Juliet didn't have would be well spent. My husband and I vowed to use every tool at hand as an opportunity to give back or a way to make life better for people. They are all human beings with one short time on Earth.[41]

Young & Rubicam CEO Ann Fudge offered a different point of view, noting: "*Struggle and tough experiences ultimately fashion you. Don't worry about the challenges. Embrace them. Go through them even if they hurt. Tell yourself, there is something to be learned from the experience. I may not fully understand it now, but I will later. It's all part of life, and life is a process of learning. Every challenging experience develops your core of inner strength, which gets you through those storms. Nothing worth doing in life is going to be easy.*[42]

5. Storms help you relate to others who have been through storms
If you desire to do good, be Great, you will have to endure a few storms so you can relate to others in the storms. Credibility is earned when you can look someone in the eye and say, "I understand . . . I've been there." Trust me, people will know if you're really genuine and authentic when you can speak from experience and not just theory.

When you have experienced the trauma of enduring a storm and come out on the end, it gives you the ability to assist others with the hope and confidence that they too not only can survive the storm, but also thrive because of the storm.

6. Storms assist you in focusing on what really matters
Virgin Mobile USA CEO Dan Schulman described how his sister's death transformed his attitude toward leadership.

Before my sister died, I was focused on moving up in AT&T. I was upwardly oriented and insecure. Often I took credit that wasn't mine to claim. My sister's death was the first time I had been dealt a giant blow. I loved her immensely. When death happens so young and cuts a life short, a lot of things you thought were important aren't important at all. When she died, I decided, "I am going to be who I am." I wanted to spend more time with my folks and my brother, rather than moving up the corporate ladder.

At that point I didn't care if I got credit for anything and became quick to credit everyone else. As team leader, I focused only on getting the job done in the best way. As a result, our teams became much more functional than they were before. All of a sudden, my career started to shoot up.[43]

Dan Schulman learned the key of storms. Storms help us focus on the real priorities of life. For this reason alone, we should embrace and accept the purpose of storms, which reveals the people and things that are really important.

When Tammi and I huddled up together in our little house in Edmond with her sister, Tia, I was not thinking about our stuff. Instead, I was holding on to the most important priority in my life—people, not things. Let the storms come into our lives so we can reevaluate the people who are priceless and the real reason for living—people.

7. Storms don't last forever

In most cases, the storms of life will pass. Certainly, there are many cases in which people have situations they must accept and deal with their entire lives. My heart and prayers go out to those people. However, for most people, storms will come and go, and the good news is that the storms will one day end. Endurance and perseverance are the very attributes that you will need to one day see the clouds go away and see the sunshine again.

I've always said, "You're either in a storm, coming out of a storm, or getting ready to face a storm." No matter what your season may be, you can be assured there is an eternal purpose for your storm. People who learn the key of dancing in the rain when the storms of life come will be better, stronger, and happier.

Reflecting on his brush with bankruptcy, Jon Huntsman commented, "At the end of the day, the creditors were our salvation. Building goodwill, being honest and kind, and paying your bills along life's pathway come back to serve you when you're down and out."

There are times in our lives when we have to ask ourselves, are we going to let this erosion of our life happen, or are we going to step up and change it? Your life speaks for itself. If I had tried to cheat somebody during my lifetime or did not play by the rules, they would have exercised their natural rights when I got in trouble. The human heart and human soul have an enormous amount of capacity to change direction in a positive way if we just keep outsiders from influencing what we're doing.[44]

Questions for you on ....
Chapter 9: Do Good, Be Great When Life Sends a Storm

1. When you read about Martin Luther King, what are some of the do good be great qualities you see?

2. Pick out one of the quotes from Martin Luther King and discuss why this particular quote inspires you.

3. What are some of the fears and emotions that come with the storms of life?

4. What is the biggest storm you have ever faced and how did you weather the storm?

5. Have you ever encountered a friend or co-worker who did not survive a storm? What lessons could you learn from their tragedy?

6. Storms reveal the real you. When you were faced with a recent storm, what came out of you that you liked, disliked?

Notes

Great Quotes from a Great Leader
Malala Yousafzai

- *"If one man can destroy everything, why can't one girl change it?"*
- *"We were scared, but our fear was not as strong as our courage."*
- *"Education is education. We should learn everything and then choose which path to follow. Education is neither eastern nor western, it is human."*
- *"If people were silent nothing would change."*
- *"There are two powers in the world; one is the sword and the other is the pen. There is a third power stronger than both; that of women."*
- *"The important thing is God has given me my life."*
- *"I was a girl in a land where rifles are fired in celebration of a son, while daughters are hidden away."*
- *"God won't give you marks if you don't work hard; God showers us with his blessings, but he is honest as well."*

10

Good Together – Do Good, Be Great With a Tribe

KEY 10: BEYOND ORDINARY PEOPLE
TRAVEL THROUGH LIFE WITH A TRIBE

Many people with good intentions of do good, be Great try to live lives of compassion and goodness in isolation and seclusion. They single-handedly try to solve large issues like poverty, hunger, or illiteracy by themselves, in silos. Our good deeds gain momentum when we realize that we don't have to try to do it all alone. Developing key partners, agencies, and colleagues will give you the power to forge ahead with boldness and confidence so that you can foster lasting change in others. People who walk through life with a tribe have a better chance of avoiding fatigue, burnout, and discouragement, because they have made the wise choice of teaming up with others to do good, be Great.

Malala Yousafzai defied the forces of the Taliban in Pakistan and helped to liberate millions of young women because she learned the power of the tribe.

MALALA YOUSAFZAI—Do Good, Be Great for Those Who Are Enslaved

Being targeted for assassination by the Taliban and becoming the youngest person in history to win the Nobel Peace Prize are not life experiences most eighteen-year-olds can lay claim to.

Pakistani teenager Malala Yousafzai can.

She was a fifteen-year-old schoolgirl on October 9, 2012, when a Taliban gunman boarded her school bus in Pakistan's Swat valley, asked for her by name, and then shot her once in the head.

Three years before that—at the age of eleven—she had started writing an anonymous blog for BBC Urdu expressing her heartfelt views on education at a time when the Taliban was destroying scores of girls schools across her valley. As the repression increasingly took control of the area, Taliban edicts were issued banning television and music, forbidding women from shopping, and limiting women's education. But Malala only grew more vocal about the right of girls to receive an education.

In 2009, a *New York Times* documentary about Malala brought her to the world's attention, and honors started to follow: In 2011, she received Pakistan's first National Youth Peace Prize and was nominated by Archbishop Desmond Tutu for the International Children's Peace Prize.

Due to the increased attention, her identity as the author of the BBC blog was revealed. Combined with her strident criticism of the Pakistani Taliban, that resulted in a vote by the radical Islamists to have her killed for being a symbol of "infidels and obscenity."

Malala said the hands of the young gunman (she estimated him to be in his early twenties) were shaking in the final moments before he pulled the trigger. The bullet hit her left brow but did not penetrate her skull. It traveled below the skin the length of the side of her head and exited into her shoulder. Critically wounded, Malala underwent surgery in Pakistan before receiving more specialized treatment in the United Kingdom, where she was discharged on January 3, 2013.

Meanwhile, the assassination attempt had backfired. It was condemned worldwide and caused protests across Pakistan. More than 2 million people signed the Right to Education petition, and Pakistan's first right to education bill was ratified. Respect for the brave young activist only grew.

In 2014 she received the Nobel Peace Prize, becoming the youngest laureate in the award's history. That year she was named one of *Time* magazine's most influential people. She also won the European Parliament's Sakharov prize for Freedom of Thought.

"It feels like this life is not my life," she said in an interview with ABC. "It's a second life. People have prayed to God to spare me and I was spared for a reason—to use my life for helping people."

Today Malala advocates for millions of girls being denied a formal education because of social, economic, legal, and political factors. Her Malala Fund empowers girls through quality secondary education to achieve their potential and create positive changes in their communities.

Specifically, her international campaign:

- Highlights what works in girls' education and calls on leaders to do more.
- Advocates at all government levels for changes that give girls access to quality community education.
- Invests in nonprofits that offer girls in the most deprived areas of the world a quality secondary education.

The fund also invests directly in lives by backing local and international secondary education initiatives. It works in six countries where adolescent girls are facing some of the most dire crises of our time:

1. Pakistan—where girls are under threat of the Taliban.
2. Nigeria—where Boko Haram is kidnapping girls en masse.
3. Jordan—where a destabilized Middle East has filled refugee camps.
4. Lebanon—where girls are in refugee camps.
5. Sierra Leone—where girls are affected by the Ebola crisis.
6. Kenya—where technology skills are needed for girls to get ahead.

In her autobiography, *I Am Malala*, released in 2013, Malala expresses her vision of what the fund can do: "The Malala Fund believes that each girl, and boy, has the power to change the world, and that all she needs is a chance"—and what it does do: "To give girls this chance, the fund aspires to invest in efforts that empower local communities, develop innovative solutions that build upon traditional approaches, and deliver not just basic literacy but the tools, ideas and networks that can help girls find their voice and build a better tomorrow."

The loss of educational opportunity is a subject that hits close to home for Malala. Her own mother was never formally educated, having grown up in a part of the world where the gender gap in education is extremely wide. Amazingly, she was due to start learning to read and write on the day Malala was shot.

Malala's power to do good, be Great began with a personal choice. On her own, she took the first brave step to break the force of repression—before she had the many supporters she has today. As she told Jon Stewart in an interview for *The Daily Show*: "Why shall I wait for someone else? . . . Why don't I raise my voice? Why don't we speak up for our rights?"

Malala's courageous refusal to back down from what she believes was vindicated on April 29, 2015, when a Pakistani antiterrorism court in her home area of Swat convicted ten Taliban men for their roles in planning the near-fatal attack on Malala. Each was sentenced to prison for twenty-five years—a life term in Pakistan.

Malala's passionate defiance of intolerance and violent extremism has succeeded in illuminating the plight of millions of children around the world who are denied an education. In advocating for them, she believes they are entitled to the same rights she claims for herself and continues to stand for. Says Malala: "I have the right of education. I have the right to play. I have the right to sing. I have the right to talk. I have the right to go to market. And I have the right to speak up."

The Key of Synergy and the Tribe
Summit Church, a Church of Do Good, Be Great

In December 2014, we received a call that would overwhelm our board and staff and really speak to the power of working together to do good, be Great. Over the previous ten years we had worked together with a very influential church in the Central Florida community, Summit Church. This church has had a dramatic influence in the Orlando area. In fact, we still feel their influence each day at our charity on 150 West Michigan Street.

Every person we touch every day receives our thumbprint of compassion. I could say more about this wonderful relationship we have with Summit Church, but this front-page article from the *Orlando Sentinel* in January of 2015 does a great job describing how we do good, be Great together.

Church's Offering is "Miracle" for Charity that Serves Hundreds in Need Each Day

While many of us were just beginning to face the debt of Christmas past this week, Pastor Scott George of the Community Food and Outreach Center in Orlando was depositing his charity's rather hefty Christmas present—a check for $65,000.

"This was a miracle and totally out of the blue," George said. "It made our year."

The windfall came from a special Christmas Eve offering taken up by Summit Church—an organization that began 12 years ago with a handful of worshipers in an apartment clubhouse. It now has some 3,000 adults who regularly attend one of its four locations.

And every year, the holiday's special offering goes to work outside the church.

"It's something we love to do," Pastor Garry Abbott said. "We want to remind everyone that we at Summit care as much about what's happening outside the walls of the church as we do about what's happening inside."

Abbott's title, for instance, is actually "mobilization" pastor. "My job is to stand in front of the congregation and tell them to get up and do something," he said. For Summit, the latest act of generosity comes just more than a year after congregants mourned the tragic death of one its founders—the troubled, charismatic Isaac Hunter, 36, who killed himself.

"That they could do so much for others, despite their own grief, is what really touched us," George said.

At least twice a year the church also offers its members the chance to roll up their sleeves and volunteer at a selected nonprofit near their church location. Typically, from 1,200 to 1,500 people enlist. For those from the

Herndon campus near Fashion Square Mall, the charity of choice has often been the Community Food and Outreach Center, which mainly helps the working poor and recently unemployed.

There, those in need can find emergency food, medical care, clothing, low-cost groceries, job training, counseling and help applying for government benefits and jobs.

More than 525 people come to the center every day for help.

"Our demand is through the roof," said George, the nonprofit's founder. "Most days, the food and aid go out as fast as they come in . . . . We live by faith that we'll be able to take care of everyone who comes to us."

Volunteers from Summit have cleaned, stocked shelves, bagged groceries and done other chores to keep the sprawling organization running smoothly. The church's middle- and high-school students have spent summers working there in lieu of attending Bible camp.

"The amount of manpower they need is huge," said Elizabeth Cronlund, Summit's community development coordinator. "It was wonderful to dedicate the offering to them, but if there are not volunteers to make that money go further, we haven't finished the job. We believe service is the opportunity to build a relationship."[45]

Good Samaritans Who Do Good, Be Great

A few years ago, *Time* magazine named three very prominent famous people as their *Time* magazine people of the year. They happened to pick three unlikely compassionate figures who, at first glance, have nothing in common, yet after closer consideration, are very similar. Bill Gates (founder of Microsoft, the largest software company in the world), his wife, Melinda Gates, and Bono from the world famous rock group U2.

On the surface, these three don't seem to have any commonality, but then you see it in their voices of compassion and actions that speak louder than words. It wasn't the picture of them on the front cover of *Time* magazine as people of the year that caught my attention; it was the caption beneath their picture: "The Good Samaritans." My first reaction was to ask, "How is this possible for a billionaire computer geek and his wife and a world famous rock star?" My initial thought was that Good Samaritan titles are reserved for popes or men or women of the clergy. *How inappropriate to name these secular icons as Good Samaritans!* I thought. Only when I read the article and heard the passion of their hearts did I quickly conclude that I had been remarkably ignorant about the profile of a Good Samaritan. I quickly learned the true heart of these people was reflected best in their words, works, and actions. Those living beyond ordinary lives possess these qualities expressed in the *Time* magazine article that changed my perspective and so much more. Let's take a minute to discover together the attributes needed to be a Good Samaritan. Then let's make the decision to apply the keys the Good Samaritan lived out—to make them a part of our everyday lives.

The Parable of the Good Samaritan

On one occasion an expert in the law stood up to test Jesus. "Teacher," he asked, "what must I do to inherit eternal life?" "What is written in the Law?" he replied. "How do you read it?"

He answered, "'Love the Lord your God with all your heart and with all your soul and with all your strength and with all your mind'; and, 'Love your neighbor as yourself.'" "You have answered correctly," Jesus replied. "Do this and you will live." But he wanted to justify himself, so he asked Jesus, "And who is my neighbor?" In reply Jesus said: "A man was going down from Jerusalem to Jericho, when he was attacked by robbers. They stripped him of his clothes, beat him and went away, leaving him half dead. A priest happened to be going down the same road, and when he saw the man, he passed by on the other side. So too, a Levite, when he came to the place and saw him, passed by on the other side. But a Samaritan, as he traveled, came where the man was; and when he saw him, he took pity on him. He went to him and bandaged his wounds, pouring on oil and wine. Then he put the man on his own donkey, brought him to an inn and took care of him. The next day he took out two denarii[c] and gave them to the innkeeper. 'Look after him,' he said, 'and when I return, I will reimburse you for any extra expense you may have.' "Which of these three do you think was a neighbor to the man who fell into the hands of robbers?" The expert in the law replied, "The one who had mercy on him." Jesus told him, "Go and do likewise." (Luke 10:25-37, NIV)

The road the man traveled that day had a reputation for being a dangerous place. Although many people had to travel on that road, each traveler was on edge and knew the risks. The road was called "bloody pass" because of the terror and pain it caused those who walked it. It wasn't a large road or wide, and its cliffs presented a perfect place for robbers to hide before ambushing the wealthy businessmen who traveled from Jerusalem to Jericho. Robbers and criminals of that day knew it well.

One day, a Jewish man was on his way to Jericho after a long day of business in Jerusalem when the robbers seized upon the moment and jumped him, ultimately leaving him nearly dead. The religious leader of that day saw the man left for dead, but then looked at his daily activity schedule and made the decision to pass him by. The Levite, an apprentice to the priest, also saw the man in need and made the decision to pass him by, as did his mentor. But the Samaritan, who by custom was not allowed to talk or interact with the Jewish man, crossed over to the other side and helped the man in need.

The Good Samaritan and His Tribe

The Good Samaritan knew down deep he couldn't help this man alone. Yet he knew the power to do good, be Great, and the impact it would have on this man who was hurting. Partnership and collaboration most likely were not in his vocabulary, but he practiced these principles and it worked beautifully. There is not much dialogue between the Good Samaritan and the innkeeper except the promise given by the Good Samaritan to come back and pay him for all the services the innkeeper provided.

The story doesn't say how long the Jewish man stayed at the inn or what services were provided, but I suspect the innkeeper knew the man would require help from the entire village, and he worked with multiple people to bring total wholeness to the man found on the side of the road. I'm sure he brought in a medical team, a team to counsel him, and a team to get him ready to return to the marketplace after his recovery. The innkeeper had the ability to attract others and work with others to bring about total restoration. The innkeeper didn't feel like he had to do it alone; he was honored and motivated to see other people's gifts and talents rise to the surface so that the Jewish man could be fully healed and restored.

Benefits of Working with a Tribe

"A tribe is a group of people connected to one another, connected to a leader, and connected to an idea. For millions of years, human beings have been part of one tribe or another. A group needs only two things to be a tribe: a shared interest and a way to communicate." [46]

1. Tribes Boost Confidence

There is a power in numbers. When you are a part of a bigger picture, it breeds confidence and boldness. John Donne said, "No man is an island entire of itself; every man is a piece of the continent, a part of the main." When you are part of a tribe, you can find strength and comfort instead of weakness and fear.

2. Tribes Boost Inspiration

You will find great inspiration when you travel through life with a loyal tribe.

Associate only with positive, focused people who you can learn from and who will not drain your valuable energy with uninspiring attitudes. By developing relationships with those committed to constant improvement and the pursuit of the best that life has to offer, you will have plenty of company on your path to the top of whatever mountain you seek to climb.
(Robin Sharma)

Loneliness in Leadership
Dr. Daniel Boorstin, Librarian of the Library of Congress, brought out a little blue box from a small closet that once held the library's rarities. The label on the box read: CONTENTS OF THE PRESIDENT'S POCKETS ON THE NIGHT OF APRIL 14, 1865. Since that was the fateful night Abraham Lincoln was assassinated, every viewer's attention was seized.

Boorstin then proceeded to remove the items in the small container and display them on camera. There were five things in the box:

- A handkerchief, embroidered "A. Lincoln"
- A country boy's penknife
- A spectacles case repaired with string
- A purse containing a $5 bill—*Confederate money (!)*
- Some old and worn newspaper clippings

"The clippings," said Boorstin, "were concerned with the great deeds of Abraham Lincoln. And one of them actually reports a speech by John Bright which says that Abraham Lincoln is 'one of the greatest men of all times.'"[47]

3. Tribes Boost Ambitions
Here is some wisdom from Mark Twain:

Keep away from people who try to belittle your ambitions. Small people always do that, but the really great make you feel that you too, can become great. When you are seeking to bring big plans to fruition, it is important with whom you regularly associate. Hang out with friends who are like-minded and who are also designing purpose-filled lives. Similarly be that kind of a friend for your friends. (Mark Twain)

"Great people talk about ideas;
Average people talk about things;
Small people talk about other people." [48]

4. Tribes Boost Connections and Open Doors

Real tribe members will connect you and help open doors for you that you could not open on your own. The people you serve and desire to help count on you to make new connections and open up doors that have been closed. Your tribe will help you connect and walk through open doors.

> *"As we grow up, we realize it is less important to have lots of friends, and more important to have real ones."* (Amanda McRae)

5. Tribes Boost Your Personal Giftings and Abilities

Hans F Hansen has said, "People inspire you, or they drain you—pick them wisely." Your tribe will inspire you. You can accomplish so much more by allowing your tribe to pull out the best in you and come alongside you to compliment your weakness. Your tribe has your back, so you can soar with your strengths and know your weakness is covered.

6. Tribes Boost Your Sustainability

Solomon once said: *"Two are better than one . . . . If either of them falls down, one can help the other up. But pity anyone who falls and has no one to help them up"* (Ecclesiastes 4:9-10, NIV). If you choose to live alone without a tribe, you will not survive and your desire to help others will not be sustainable.

Live with a tribe of trusted friends so that when you fall you can get back up by their help and encouragement. As Oprah Winfrey says, "Surround yourself with only people who are going to lift you higher."

7. Tribes Boost Your Dreams

"Surround yourself with people who believe in your dreams." (Website:*heallovebe.files.wordpress.com*)

Surround yourself with a tribe that boosts and believes in your dreams. Not everyone is supposed to be in your tribe. The key to living beyond ordinary is selecting those few people who can make you feel better and help you fulfill your dreams as you help them fulfill their dreams.

Why Don't We Embrace a Tribe and Work Great Together?

There are many reasons why we seem to operate in silos. It's rare to find churches and nonprofits in our communities that are willing to drop the walls of division and competition in order to bring healing and restoration to families and people in need.

Here are a few reasons why we don't work together to do good, be Great:

1. **Ego**—Pride is the main reason we choose not to travel through life with a tribe. We convince ourselves that we are just fine and don't need anyone or anything from others. How lonely this must be to live isolated, alone, and full of ego and pride.

2. **Money**—Most people choose to live on an island because they are afraid that they will not be supported if they operate with a team.

3. **Who will get the credit?**—Who will get the credit? This is the ultimate question people who resist the tribe methodology ask themselves. They are not really concerned about getting people in need help; they are more concerned about who will get the recognition and credit for it.

4. **There's comfort working in silos**—When you live without a tribe, your attention moves from others to yourself. Many people find great comfort in working alone and in silos. They only have to think about themselves and many people find life easier with their eyes on themselves than on others.

5. **Working with others can be challenging**—People can be difficult at times. Working in a tribe means you have to sometimes let go of your ideas and opinions. People are a challenge at times, but when you learn the key of getting along, much can be accomplished.

Tribe Busters

Jim Rohn once said, "You are the average of the five people you spend the most time with." When you are traveling in your tribe you must be very careful who you pick and choose to be in it. If even one person in your tribe is not on the same page, it can bring disunity and friction, which is unnecessary. These are "tribe busters." These are the people to avoid or from which you must stay away. I'm very selective in regard to who I want in my tribe. You too should be careful who to embrace and who to avoid:

1. **Promise Breakers**
    Avoid people who you cannot trust and who cannot keep their word. They will destroy the spirit of trust needed for a healthy tribe.
2. **One-Uppers**
    People who always have to one-up and continually try to elevate themselves above you and others will sadly bring division and discord into your tribe.
3. **Dream Killers**
    Some people are gifted at killing the hope and dreams of others. They usually have no dreams of their own, but wake up each morning ready to squash any dream into which they come in contact.
4. **Faultfinders**
    These toxic people can never find fault in themselves, but have a gifting for exposing your faults and issues. Avoid them like the plague.
5. **Joy Suckers**
    Nothing is worse than hanging around people who are grumpy and scrooges. They are mad at the world and will suck all the joy out of you if you let them.
6. **Life Drainers**
    Don't pick people for your tribe who do not motivate you and inspire you. Some people just drain the life out of you with their constant problems and issues. They have new problems every day and they are looking for others to dump them on. Don't let the life drainers sap you of your precious energy.

QUESTIONS FOR YOU ON ....
CHAPTER 10: GOOD TOGETHER - DO GOOD, BE GREAT
WITH A TRIBE

1. When you read about Malala Yousafzai, what are some of the do good be great qualities you see?

2. Pick out one of the quotes from Malala Yousafzai and discuss why this particular quote inspires you.

3. Describe your tribe. Who are they and what qualities do they bring to you that help you be great?

4. How did the Good Samaritan apply the "tribe principle" to do good great?

5. List out some of the benefits of traveling with a tribe.

6. What are a few of the enemies of a tribe? How do they destroy your tribe?

Notes

Great Quotes from a Great Leader
Jesus Christ

- *"If you want to be perfect, go, sell your possessions and give to the poor, and you will have treasure in heaven" (Matt 19:21, NIV).*
- *"Blessed are the merciful: for they shall obtain mercy" (Matt 5:7, NIV).*
- *"Blessed are the peacemakers: for they shall be called the children of God" (Matt 5:9, NIV).*
- *"And if you greet only your brothers, what are you doing more than others? Do not even pagans do that?" (Matt 5:47, NIV).*
- *What good will it be for a man if he gains the whole world, yet forfeits his soul? (Matt 16:26, NIV).*
- *"Make a tree good and its fruit will be good, or make a tree bad and its fruit will be bad, for a tree is recognized by its fruit" (Matt 12:33, NIV).*
- *"Love the Lord your God with all your heart and with all your soul and with all your strength and with all your mind; and, Love your neighbor as yourself " (Luke 10:27, NIV).*
- *"It is not the healthy who need a doctor, but the sick. I have not come to call the righteous, but sinners" (Mark 2:17, NIV).*
- *"A new command I give you: Love one another. As I have loved you, so you must love one another" (John 13:34, NIV).*
- *"Blessed are the poor in spirit, for theirs is the kingdom of heaven" (Matt 5:3, NIV)*

11

Good To Go – Do Good, Be Great Starts With You and Starts Now

KEY 11: BEYOND ORDINARY PEOPLE BELIEVE IN THE FORCE OF NOW

JESUS—Do Good, Be Great for Those Who Need Abundant Life

Jesus (*Yeshua* in Hebrew) was born in Israel more than 2,000 years ago. He was a Jew, and for His first thirty years, He lived a traditional Jewish life. As an adult He earned His living as a carpenter.

During His lifetime, Israel was controlled by the Roman Empire. Rome's occupying forces ruled it with an iron hand, and the edicts of Caesar's dictatorship were the law of the land, including in Bethlehem, where Jesus was born, and Nazareth, where He was raised.

At about age thirty, Jesus began His public ministry. It lasted only about three years, during which time He worked miracles that were documented in writing by eyewitnesses. He was accompanied by twelve Jewish men from a variety of backgrounds whom He personally discipled. A larger close-knit group which also included women, was part of His extended group of disciples. He walked the southern and northern regions of Israel, but never traveled more than 200 miles from His birthplace. Still, His reputation spread nationwide.

The Pharisees and Sadducees who embodied the ruling religious counsels of the Jewish people, kept a close eye on Him. He posed a threat to their authority because His public teachings and miracles often called into question the integrity of their leadership.

The key messages in Jesus' teachings include:

- Good news: the kingdom of God has come to earth.
- God loves us.
- We are to love others in the same way we love ourselves.
- Each person is of immense value to God.
- Each person is separated from God by sin.
- God sent Jesus, His only Son, to save the world from its sin.
- God commands all people everywhere to repent and be restored to God.
- He has set a day when He will judge the world by Jesus.
- The proof of all of the above is that God raised Jesus from the dead.
- Jesus will forgive, accept, and not turn away anyone who comes to Him.

During His three years of ministry, Jesus went about doing good and healing all who were oppressed by the devil. He healed all kinds of sicknesses and disease. Some of His most remarkable actions included:

- Turning water into wine at a Hebrew wedding (John 2:1-11).
- Healing a royal official's son (John 4:46-54).
- Healing a man crippled for thirty-eight years (John 5:1-9).
- Feeding more than 5,000 people with five loaves and two fish (John 6:1-14).
- Walking on water (John 6:16-21).
- Healing a man born blind (John 9:1-7).
- Raising Lazarus from the dead after four days in the grave (John 11:17-44).

Not surprisingly, a common question surrounding Jesus during His ministry was, "Who is this Jesus, really?" His most controversial teaching was that He repeatedly claimed to be the Son of God. The Jews who believed in Him called Him the Messiah, from which is derived the Greek word *Christ*, meaning "anointed one."

Claiming to be God's Son was a direct violation of Jewish blasphemy law, and punishable by death. The Jewish religious leaders, after arresting Jesus, convicted Him during an illegally convened nighttime trial, and took Him to the Roman rulers to have Him executed.

However, in each of several hearings conducted by separate Roman officials, Jesus was found innocent of breaking any Roman law. Eventually the religious leaders, unable to prevail before the authorities, prompted a near riot among the people loyal to them, which persuaded the Roman governor, Pilate, that the execution of one man was preferable to unrest in Jerusalem. Jesus was condemned to death by Pilate, and brutally beaten, tortured, and whipped before being nailed by His hands and feet to a wooden cross.

According to more than 500 witnesses, Jesus rose from the dead three days later, and over the next forty days appeared to many in both the southern and northern provinces of Israel. As a result of these miraculous events, the number of His followers rapidly increased. A few months later in Jerusalem, according to an eyewitness named Luke, some 3,000 new followers were added in a single day.

The subsequent spread of Jesus' message throughout the Roman Empire was often met with force, and many of His followers chose to die rather than deny their belief in Him as the Son of God. In just over 300 years, Christianity became the official religion of the Roman Empire.

The following excerpt from nineteenth century author James Allan Francis's, *One Solitary Life*, illuminates the remarkable change in the world that Jesus made to do good, be Great:

He was born in an obscure village, the child of a peasant woman. Until He was thirty, He worked in a carpenter shop and then for three years He was an itinerant preacher. He wrote no books. He held no office. He never owned a home. He never did any of the things that usually accompany greatness. The authorities condemned His teachings. His friends deserted

Him. One betrayed Him to His enemies for a paltry sum. One denied Him. He went through the mockery of a trial. He was nailed on a cross between two thieves. While He was dying, His executioners gambled for the only piece of property He owned on earth: His coat. When He was dead He was taken down and placed in a borrowed grave. Nineteen centuries have come and gone, yet all the armies that ever marched and all the navies that were ever assembled and all the parliaments that ever sat and all the rulers that ever reigned have not affected humanity upon this earth so profoundly as that one solitary life.

Jesus' original words and deeds, as recorded by His followers, can be found in the Bible and still speak loudly for themselves.

Delbert & Sandy Groves—Do Good, Be Great in Zambia

I have found over the years that most times when requests are inconvenient, those times are usually the moments that seem to be the most productive. This was certainly the case. So with deadlines and a schedule to meet with editing and production, when it would have been easy to dismiss this chance, I said, "Yes," even though it may not have made sense or seemed like the most logical choice.

On this international trip, I met and interviewed two very special people who are doing an amazing job and living beyond ordinary lives. The invite came from these two missionaries who have served the people of Zambia for twenty-five years, Delbert and Sandy Groves. The Groves were living a very nice and comfortable life in Orlando, Florida. Delbert was a printer by trade and very easily could have "settled in" to the American Dream of building his career, raising a family, and saving for his retirement. It would have been tempting to accept this and live the "good life." But Delbert and Sandy realized they were created with a special purpose and destiny. They were discontent with good, average, or ordinary. They felt a sense of urgency and friction and knew that life was short; that you only live once.

Challenged by an inner call and unsettled feeling in their hearts, they made the gut-wrenching decision to leave it all in the US and go to Africa to live beyond ordinary lives. Their personal decision to do good, be Great cost them everything, but they have gained the priceless gift of significance, purpose, and destiny by following their hearts and faith. I'm sure it was difficult and painful. I'm confident that they thought many times of quitting and giving up. I know that there were seasons of defeat, discouragement, and depression. No one accomplishes what they have done without facing the enemies that thrive on trying to keep you and me living the "status quo" life—a life in the "comfort zone."

To look at Delbert and Sandy, you would think they were the typical suburban US couple. Nothing would strike you as extraordinary in their appearance, mannerisms, or personality, but nothing could be further from the truth. They are an amazing couple that has lived a life of service to the continent of Africa; hundreds of thousands of people in Zambia and beyond have been inspired and helped by their beyond ordinary lives.

The New Life Center, which they established outside of Kitwe, Zambia, seems from the outside like the typical campus for missionaries. It includes a small and modest home, guest home for visitors, classrooms for a teacher and students, computer labs, and church building with large kitchen for feeding programs. It's a beautiful and well-kept campus—an amazing place that brings help and hope to the citizens of Kitwe. In the back of the property is a large metal shed that doesn't look like much, but it houses one of the most amazing outreaches I have ever seen. This fifty foot by one hundred fifty foot metal building houses a dynamic vision that gives Delbert and Sandy a beyond ordinary ministry. It is the "plaza" where they have moved from good to Great, where they have learned the key of living the life most people dream of.

Delbert had taken me on the usual tour of the compound after I arrived. I was impressed with the staff, the buildings, and the culture they have created in Zambia, but my heart really began to beat faster as we approached this metal building that I had heard about from so many people in Central Florida. Hundreds of people had told me that I had to see this place. Many of them know my heart for giving hand ups to people in Orlando and around the world. So as we approached the building, my anticipation grew and grew.

A small sign outside identified it as the PET building. PET stands for Personal Empowerment Transportation. Delbert, Sandy, and their staff have built fantastic, small bicycles designed to be powered by hand. They are for people who are crippled, paralyzed, or have no legs. Because of these simple yet powerful machines, thousands of people who otherwise would be immobile and stationary are now liberated and given newfound freedom. The warehouse was filled with hundreds of these PETs that we would load up and deliver to a distant village in a few days as part of our pastoring conference.

I am woefully incapable of explaining either in person or through written word the absolutely overwhelming experience it was for me to observe the lame, crippled, paralyzed, and physically challenged men, women and children as they literally crawl on the dirt ground to get into the PET and experience the joy of mobility.

The people of Zambia are very fortunate to have such visionaries and amazing leaders as Delbert and Sandy Groves. Their countries and the continent of Africa are living the key to living beyond ordinary, to do good, be Great.

So, let's look at how we can live the keys of living a life of service and compassion.

How Do I Begin To Do Good, Be Great?

1. Start Small
In his book, *Fast Living: How the Church Will End Extreme Poverty*, Scott C. Todd beautifully describes how you can start to do good, be Great by starting small:

In the late twentieth century, there was a story written by Loren Eiseley called, *"The Star Thrower"* that became popular among Christians. It goes like this:

A man was walking along the beach when he saw a boy picking something up and throwing it into the ocean.

Approaching the boy, he asked, "What are you doing?"

"Throwing starfish back into the ocean," he said. "The surf is up and tide is going out. If I don't throw them back, they'll die."

"Son," the man said, "don't you realize there are miles and miles of beach and hundreds of starfish? You can't make a difference!"

After listening politely, the boy bent down, picked up another starfish and threw it back into the surf. Then, smiling at the man, he said, "I made a difference for that one." [49]

Had the story been written for the twenty-first century Christian, it would be quite different:

A man was walking along the beach when he saw a girl taking a picture of a starfish with her iPhone.

Approaching the girl, he asked, "What are you doing?"

"Uploading pictures of these stranded starfish to my Facebook page and asking friends to Tweet the call to action," she said. "If I can get enough friends out here, we can get all these starfish back into the water before sunset."

"Little girl," the man asked, "what does Tweet mean?"

The girl rolled her eyes. She bent down, picked up a starfish, and threw it back into the surf. Then she gave the man a wry, twinkly-eyed smile and said, "If you want to help out, this is how you do it."

Within hours, thousands of children stormed the beach and every starfish was rescued.

In *Jesus Wants to Save Christians*, Rob Bell says, "Our destiny, our future, and our joy is using whatever blessing we've received, whatever resources, talents, skills, and passions God has given us, to make the world a better place." Lao-tzu (604-531 BC) wrote, "A journey of a thousand miles must begin with a single step."

2. Start Now

We can't choose whether we will get any more time, but we can choose what we do with it. *There is an old Chinese proverb that says: "The best time to plant a tree was 20 years ago. The next best time is now."*

SOMEDAY WHEN THE KIDS ARE GROWN, things are going to be a lot different. The garage won't be full of bikes, sawhorses surrounded by chunks of two-by-fours, nails, a hammer and saw, unfinished "experimental projects," and the rabbit cage. I'll be able to park both cars neatly in just the right places, and never again stumble over skateboards, a pile of papers (saved for the school fund drive), or the bag of rabbit food, now split and spilled. **Ugh!**

SOMEDAY WHEN THE KIDS ARE GROWN, the kitchen will be incredibly neat. The sink will stay free of sticky dishes, the garbage disposal won't get choked on rubber bands or paper cups, the refrigerator won't be clogged with nine bottles of milk, and we won't lose the tops to jelly jars, catsup bottles, the peanut butter, the margarine, or the mustard. The water jar won't be put back empty, the ice trays won't be left out overnight, the blender won't stand for six hours coated with the remains of midnight malt, and the honey will stay **inside** *the container.*

YES, SOMEDAY WHEN THE KIDS ARE GROWN, things are going to be a lot different. One by one they'll leave our nest, and the place will begin to resemble order and maybe even a touch of elegance. The clink of china and silver will be heard on occasion. The crackling of the fireplace will echo through the hallway. The phone will be strangely silent. The house will be:

quiet . . .
and calm . . .
and always clean . . .
and empty . . .
and filled with memories . . .
and lonely . . .
and we won't like that at all. And we'll spend our time not looking forward to **Someday** *but looking back to* **Yesterday.**[50]

3. Start Where You Are

This message found under the lid of a Timberland shoebox in 2010 shows Timberland's commitment to do good, be Great by starting where they are.

The opportunity to make [the world] better is everywhere if we choose to act. Better is seeing a void and filling it. Hearing a call for help and answering it. Taking a wrong and making it right. It is as small as making booths, shoes and gear or as big as changing the world. Better is giving employees time to serve. Building a house. Painting a school. Empowering our youth. Feeding the hungry. Or revitalizing a community. Better is a call to action. A rallying cry. Fearless. Determined. Passionate. And connected. It is searching within. Reaching out. Heading into the eye of the storm. Adventuring out to the middle of nowhere. And doing so with purpose. So when the sun sets and we think about what tomorrow will bring, we understand that better is not what we do. It is who we are. [51]

4. Start Courageously

Every great person who desires to do good, be Great will do so with courage.

Cripple him, and you have a Sir Walter Scott. Lock him in a prison cell, and you have a John Bunyan. Bury him in the snows of Valley Forge, and you have a George Washington. Raise him in abject poverty and you have an Abraham Lincoln. Strike him down with infantile paralysis, and he becomes Franklin Roosevelt. Burn him so severely that the doctors say he'll never walk again, and you have a Glenn Cunningham—who set the world's one-mile record in 1934. Deafen him and you have a Ludwig van Beethoven. Have him or her born black in a society filled with racial discrimination, and you have a Booker T. Washington, a Marian Anderson, a George Washington Carver . . . . Call him a slow learner, "retarded," and write him off as uneducable, and you have an Albert Einstein. [52]

Max Lucado, in his book *Outlive Your Life*, urges:

"Get ticked off, riled up enough to respond. Righteous anger would do a world of good. Poverty is not the lack of charity but the lack of justice . . . . No one can do everything, but everyone can do something."

5. Start Despite Opposition

Anyone who aspires to do good, be Great will encounter opposition. Chuck Swindoll tells a great story that illustrates how opposition can motivate us to continue with boldness.

Ignace Jan Paderewski, the famous composer-pianist, was scheduled to perform at a great concert hall in America. It was an evening to remember— black tuxedos and long evening dresses, a high-society extravaganza full bore. Present in the audience that evening was a mother with her fidgety nine-year-old son. Weary of waiting, he squirmed constantly in his seat. His mother was in hopes that her boy would be encouraged to practice the piano if he could just hear the immortal Paderewski at the keyboard. So—against his wishes—he had come.

As she turned to talk with friends, her son could stay seated no longer. He slipped away from her side, strangely drawn to the ebony concert grand Steinway and its leather tufted stool on the huge stage flooded with blinding lights. Without much notice from the sophisticated audience, the boy sat down at the stool, staring wide-eyed at the black and white keys. He placed his small, trembling fingers in the right location and began to play "Chop Sticks." The roar of the crowd was hushed as hundreds of frowning faces turned in his direction. Irritated and embarrassed, they began to shout:

"Get that boy away from there!"

"Who'd bring a kid that young in here?"

"Where's his mother?"

"Somebody stop him!"

Backstage, the master overheard the sounds out front and quickly put together in his mind what was happening. Hurriedly, he grabbed his coat and rushed toward the stage. Without one word of announcement he stooped over behind the boy, reached around both sides, and began to improvise a counter melody to harmonize with and enhance "Chop Sticks." As the two of them played together, Paderewski kept whispering in the boy's ear: "Keep going. Don't quit, son. Keep on playing . . . don't stop...don't quit."[53]

6. Start Now . . . Before It's Too Late

Time is ticking; if you're not careful, you'll run out of marbles!

Don't Lose Your Marbles

If you wait until the perfect timing, you'll never get to it. Many people wait until "someday," and "someday" never comes. John Maxwell tells the story of a ham radio operator who overheard an older gentleman giving advice to a younger man:

"It's a shame you have to be away from home and family so much," he said. "Let me tell you something that has helped me keep a good perspective on my own priorities. You see, one day I sat down and did a little arithmetic. The average person lives about 75 years. Now then, I multiplied 75 times 52 and came up with 3,900, which is the number of Saturdays that the average person has in his lifetime.

"It took me until I was 55 years old to think about this in any detail," he continued, "and by that time I had lived through over 2,800 Saturdays. I got to thinking that if I lived to be 75, I only had about a thousand of them left to enjoy."

He went on to explain that he bought 1,000 marbles and put them in a clear plastic container in his favorite work area at home. "Every Saturday since then," he said, "I have taken one marble out and thrown it away. I found that by watching the marbles diminish, I focused more on the really important things in life. There's nothing like watching your time here on this earth run out to help get your priorities straight."

Then the older gentleman finished, "Now let me tell you one last thought before I sign off and take my lovely wife out to breakfast. This morning, I took the very last marble out of the container. I figure if I make it until next Saturday, then I have been given a little extra time."[54]

Women of Hope . . . Do Good, Be Great Together

Now that our children are in college and we have a little more time on our hands, maybe we could all get together and see if we can make a difference in our community. After all, she thought, *we have so much to offer and we could make a real impact in the lives of so many families in need, suffering children, and fill huge voids in our community. They are waiting on us.*

And so it started with my wife Tammi's desire to mobilize her friends and neighbors to action, to live a life of do good, be Great. What started with our next-door neighbor, Terri Mitchell, soon spread to the entire King's Row subdivision in a suburb of Maitland. It spread to a nearby suburb of Winter Park, and now it is spreading throughout our community. Women of Hope was born. This auxiliary group supports the vision and mission of Community Food and Outreach Center (CFOC).

These generous women could have very easily sat back and coasted through the next season of their life. They didn't have to get on board and give their lives away as they have. They didn't have to put the needs of others on the top of their list, but they did, and what a difference they have made. For the past five years, these dedicated women have organized their annual Hope 'n' Heel event, which has raised tens of thousands of dollars for the CFOC cause and mission. They encourage women throughout Central Florida to attend this evening of fun, laughter, and purpose. The only prerequisites are that all those who attend must wear heels and want to have a fun time filled with the underlying mission of helping families and children in need. Hundreds of women come together and enjoy great food and wine, and bid on auction items that eventually turn into opportunities to help their neighbors in need. The event, usually held in early spring, kicks off the year by raising financial support, increasing advocacy, and building relationships that will continue throughout the year in support of CFOC.

A Beyond Ordinary Encounter That Started Something Great

Our building at 150 West Michigan Street in Orlando used to be part of a lumberyard called West Lumber before we converted it into a campus of help and hope. It's not fancy, but it is filled with encouragement and acceptance.

Most guests on our campus tours are moved to tears and experience emotions of shock and disbelief. They wonder how the city could attract more tourists each year than any place on earth, yet have such a high percentage of working poor residents. They are shocked that we lead the nation in tourism, but also lead the nation in the lowest wage for employees. Of the thousands of tours I have led over the years, I certainly never had a guest who was unimpressed or angry . . . until one day.

It was a few years ago, and I was walking a few businessmen around on a tour of our campus. The tour began like most tours, and at the end of it we ended up in our cost-share grocery program area where our staff and volunteers served just a few of the hundreds of families that would visit that day. This is when a certain encounter occurred that sent things south. I did not know then the positive effect that encounter would have for years to come on thousands of families.

As I talked to the small group of businessmen, one of them suddenly turned ghost white and started shaking, visibly. My first thought was that the guest was sick, or was getting ready to be sick. The others on the tour hadn't picked up on it, but being the communicator I am, I knew instantly that I had lost the man, but didn't have a clue why. Was it something I had said? Was it something he saw? What went so wrong that he would instantly become uncomfortable and uneasy?

I tried to wrap up my presentation within the five minutes we had left. My mouth was going through the motions of my talk, but my mind was going 1,000 miles an hour trying to figure out how to rescue the moment and find out what was going on. After a few minutes, all the guests shook my hand, thanked me, and let me know how much they appreciated the tour before they left—all except one man named Dave. And after everyone else had filed out, only he and I remained. Now was my chance to find out what in the world was going on.

"Dave, what happened in there? Are you OK? What's going on?" After taking a few minutes to get his act together, he proceeded to tell me that as we finished the tour, he had looked at the people standing in line to check out at the cost-share grocery program. As he looked, he had locked eyes with one person in particular, and both had frozen in place. His eyes connected with someone in line that he had not expected to see—one of his executive assistants. Suddenly the validity of our programs and services became crystal clear, revealing the reality of our mission in an instant.

As their eyes met, the middle-aged struggling mom in line did not have to say a word. Her standing in line to get a hand up said more to him than any words could express. I didn't have to say a thing. He needed no more speeches, presentations, or persuasive sales pitches—which, by the way, rarely make the greater difference—because when people see first-hand what we do, they are overwhelmingly deeply touched and motivated to help.

He was so overwhelmed that day that he went right to his boss who happens to employ thousands of people in Florida. In an instant, Dave became our greatest advocate and cheerleader. That day, he told his boss that our mission was "taking care of *our* people." Then he told his boss, "We need to take care of Community Food and Outreach." He didn't give a long speech to his boss, but it was full of passion and action. It didn't take him and his company long to become one of our biggest corporate partners. His company donated generously and sent volunteers on a regular basis. Dave became involved in our leadership team and has made a huge impact on our community and our organization—all because he was moved to action and determined to do good, be Great.

I wish other large companies and organizations would follow in his footsteps and help us help their staff and employees stay fed, clothed, and healthy and happy. His decisive motivation to action has helped thousands of people over the years. Great things happen when you are moved to action.

Cows 'n' Cabs—A Good Event Helping Others Do Good and Be Great

He used this beyond-ordinary encounter to motivate himself and others to begin a yearly event called Cows 'n' Cabs. This fantastic event is held in October. The finest restaurants and wine retailers in the state come together in downtown Winter Park, a suburb of Orlando, to raise funds and awareness for the Community Food and Outreach Center. To date, this event has raised thousands of dollars each year, quickly becoming one of the best and most well attended charity events in Central Florida. Thousands of families have been assisted due to this beyond ordinary event that he helped create. He took a step and has made a huge difference. You can too. Just determine to make your life count to do Good and be Great.

The next few pages are perhaps the most important in the book. They represent the beginning for you in writing down your visions, dreams, and goals for living a beyond ordinary life by do good, be Great. Don't skip over this section and simply close the book and put it on your shelf. Take the next few hours, days, or months and chronicle your thoughts, ideas, hopes, visions, and dreams. This can be the start of something that will change not only you and your family, but the world as well.

After you fill in the next few pages, take a minute to write me an email at jscottgeorge1@gmail.com and let me know you are committed to a life beyond ordinary and to living your passion to do good, be Great. You will have the opportunity to view your dreams on our website, doinggoodgreat. org, and also see the dreams others have shared.

Questions for you on ....
Chapter 11: Good To Go - Do Good, Be Great Starts With You
and Starts Now

1. When you read about Jesus, what are some of the do good be great qualities you see?

2. Pick out one of the quotes from Jesus and discuss why this particular quote inspires you.

3. How does the force of "now" compare with the force of yesterday or tomorrow?

4. How do you begin doing good great now instead of someday?

5. In order to live a life of doing good great you have to start now. What have you been putting off that you need to start doing now?

6. How old are you? The average person lives only 75 years. To live a life of doing good great, what can you begin to do today that will help you to live a life of purpose and destiny?

Notes

Conclusion

The beyond ordinary life is lived by those who are determined to leave a legacy in their communities of do good, be Great, despite the odds. I'll leave you with one quote from Theodore Roosevelt's famous 1910 speech to motivate you to do good, be Great:

Theodore Roosevelt's famous 1910 speech at the Sorbonne, "*The Man in the Arena.*"

"It is not the critic who counts; not the man who points out how the strong man stumbles, or where the doer of deeds could have done them better. The credit belongs to the man who is actually in the arena, whose face is marred by dust and sweat and blood; who strives valiantly . . . who knows good enthusiasms, the great devotions; who spends himself in a worthy cause; who at the best knows in the end the triumph of high achievements, and who at the worst, if he fails, at least fails while daring greatly, so that his place shall never be with those cold and timid souls who neither know victory nor defeat."[55]

About The Author

Nonprofit pioneer, speaker, and author **Scott George** has been a passionate and compassionate visionary and innovator in the church and nonprofit world for over thirty years. His unique ability to communicate leadership principles and insights has motivated and inspired groups of all sizes. He has traveled the world, bringing hope and help everywhere he goes through philanthropic and humanitarian campaigns and outreaches. He currently serves as senior pastor of Pine Castle United Methodist Church in Orlando, FL, and is the founder of UP – United Against Poverty (formerly known as Community Food and Outreach Center) in downtown Orlando, an innovative, cutting-edge nonprofit facility that serves thousands of families each month with food, medical care, crisis intervention and education. Scott is happily married to Tammi, his wife, and has four children—Austen, Aaren, Amanda, and Allison.

Speaking and Appearances

If you would like to schedule Scott George for a speaking engagement or appearance, please call, email, or write him, using the information below:

J. Scott George; 130 Galahad Lane; Maitland, FL 32751

Websites:

www.doinggoodgreat.org
www.livingbeyondordinary.org
www.dogoodbegreat.org
www.alwaysdoinggood.com
www.jscottgeorge.com

Email: jscottgeorge1@gmail.com

Phone: 407-579-8515

Social Media: Follow Scott George on Twitter:
@RevJScottGeorge (https://twitter.com/RevJScottGeorge/)
Become a fan of Scott George on Facebook: J Scott George (https://www.
facebook.com/pages/J-scott-george/668980636525535)

Connect with Scott George on LinkedIn: J Scott George (https://www. linkedin.com/profile/view?id=237735739)

Watch Scott George on YouTube: J Scott (http://www.jscottgeorge.com/)

Watch Scott share the story of Living Beyond Ordinary: https://vimeo. com/132738501

Also by Scott George

Living Beyond Ordinary Discovering Authentic Significance and Purpose
www.livingbeyondordinary.org
"Living Beyond Ordinary is the inspirational account of how an ordinary life, fueled by an extraordinary vision, can help to change a community one life at a time."

Congressman Daniel Webster
*"I am excited Scott George has shared his experiences in his new book, **Living Beyond Ordinary: Discovering Authentic Significance and Purpose**. The story of how Scott started this charity outreach—with one pallet of food and sheer dedication and determination—is truly an inspiration. Scott's vision has motivated so many people in our community to help thousands of families obtain a better quality of life. His vision and insight is one I admire and appreciate."*

Orlando Mayor Buddy Dyer
"Orange County Florida is fortunate to have Scott George and his leadership. The Community Food and Outreach Center makes our community a better place to live."

Teresa Jacobs, Orange County Mayor
"Pastor Scott George is somewhat of a hero in our community—a man who acted out of faith and loved out of compassion. This book will not only inspire you, it will make you want to help someone . . . or even accomplish your own God-given dreams."

Also by Scott George

Doing Good, Great
11 Secrets to Living Beyond Ordinary

www.doinggoodgreat.org

Scott George has been an inspiration to me and so many in Central Florida by modeling the living out of the Gospel through "doing good" (The Great Commandment) and sharing the life-changing message of the Gospel – "good news." (The Great Commission) The Community Food & Outreach Center and Scott are shining lights in our community.
Jack McGill
President, Elevate Orlando

If anyone is qualified to give the "Secrets to Living Beyond Ordinary" it is Pastor Scott George. Scott, obviously on his own personal journey of stewardship in his community, has many uplifting and exciting stories to tell about his successes and the successful people he meets along the way. He humbly quotes others as being "wiser people" than himself; yet the wisdom he provides, and the compassion he adds to back it up, is life changing!
Bill Mills
Florida Prosperity Partnership

This book filled with powerful principles and life-changing stories will inspire a little spark of advocacy for so many in need. They show how one can take the ordinary and do unordinary work for those who are lost.
Dick Batchelor
Advocate, DBMG, Inc.

Also by Scott George

GPS: Guiding Principles for Success
Timeless Truths for Everyday Life
www.livingbeyondordinary.org
Have you ever been lost without your mobile phone or GPS? Most likely you experienced:
FEAR
PANIC
STRESS

Many people walk through life without a guiding force to help them navigate through the obstacles life brings. *GPS: Guiding Principles for Success* offers wisdom, insight, and advice from one of the wisest men of all time: Solomon.

Learn valuable life lessons that can help you become a better person, leader, or parent. You don't have to walk it alone—you can live life with confidence and courage as you use these life-giving and life-guiding principles.

Notes

1. Brian Tracy, *Focal Point* (Amacon Books, 2004)

2. Told to the author (Pat Williams) by Disney historian Paul Anderson of Brigham Young University in a telephone interview. *"Coach Wooden's Greatest Secret,"* Pat Williams with Jim Denney, Chapter 4, pg. 87.

3. "Election 2000, *"Does My Vote Really Matter?"* last modified December 6, 2000, http://www.classical-homeschooling.org/onevote.html,

4. *Helping Others Help Themselves,* spring newsletter CFOC

5. Bill George with Peter Sims, *True North* (John Wiley & Sons, Inc., 2007), xxxi, Introduction

6. Bill George with Peter Sims, *True North* (John Wiley & Sons, Inc., 2007)

7. Bill George with Peter Sims, *True North* (John Wiley & Sons, Inc., 2007), xxvi, Introduction

8. Bill George with Peter Sims, *True North* (John Wiley & Sons, Inc., 2007), 5

9. Dr. David Jeremiah, *What Are You Afraid Of?* (Tyndale House, 2013)

10. "The World Needs Men," *poem by Ted Engstrom,* posted on January 29, 2013, http://actlikeaman.org/2013/01/world-men/

11. "BrainyQuote, Shari Arison Quotes," 2001 - 2015 BrainyQuote, accessed June 30, 2015, http://www.brainyquote.com/quotes/quotes/s/shariariso645272.html

12. "Risking," Greatest-Inspirational-Quotes, accessed June 30, 2015, http://www.greatest-inspirational-quotes.com/risk-appearing-the-fool.html

13. "Wikipedia, *Kairos*," last modified July 20, 2015, https://en.wikipedia.org/wiki/Kairos

14. Pat Williams with Jim Denny, *Coach Wooden's Greatest Secret* (Revell, a division of Baker Publishing Group, 2014), 114

15. Timothy J. Keller, *Ministries of Mercy: The Call of the Jericho Road* (P & R Publishing; 2nd edition (July 1, 1997)

16. Pat Williams with Jim Denny, *Coach Wooden's Greatest Secret* (Revell, a division of Baker Publishing Group, 2014), 150-157

17. Steve Corbett and Brian Fikkert, *When Helping Hurts* (Moody Publishers, 2009)

18. "Don't Try to Manage Your Time-Manage Yourself," The John Maxwell Co., May 26, 2015, http://www.johnmaxwell.com/blog/dont-try-to-manage-your-time-manage-yourself

19. Norman Vincent Peale, Norman Vincent Peale, *Positive Thinking: The Norman Vincent Peale Story* (Public broadcasting, 2006)

20. Bob Lupton, *Toxic Charity* (Harper One Publishing, 2011)

21. "From Hunger to Health; The Oath for Compassionate Service," Bob Lupton, accessed June 2015, http://hungerintohealth.com/2012/10/16/toxic-charity-how-service-organizations-hurt-those-they-help-and-how-to-reverse-it/

22. Bob Lupton, *Toxic Charity* (Harper One Publishing, 2011)

23. Bob Lupton, *Toxic Charity* (HarperOne Publishing, 2011)

24. Pat Williams with Jim Denny, *Coach Wooden's Greatest Secret: The Power of a Lot of Little Things Done Well*, (Revell, a division of Baker Publishing Group, Grand Rapids, MI, 2014), 140

25. Edith Schaeffer, *What Is a Family?* (Old Tappan, N.J.: Fleming H. Revell, 1975), 119

26. Bill George with Peter Sims, *True North* (John Wiley & Sons, Inc., 2007), xxiv, Introduction

27. "Quote by John Maxwell," John C. Maxwell Quotes, accessed 7/30/15, 2015 Goodreads, http://www.goodreads.com/quotes/166588-image-is-what-people-think-we-are-integrity-is-whar

28. Leo Rangell, M.D., *The Mind of Watergate* (New York: W.W. Norton & Company, 1980), 24-25

29. *Optimize Magazine (Information Week's* monthly publication for corporate investment officers) May 2005 issue

30. Pat Williams with Jim Denney, *Coach Wooden's Greatest Secret: The Power of a Lot of Little Things Done Well* (Revell, a division of Baker Publishing Group, Grand Rapids, MI, 2014) 138-139

31. Pat Williams with Jim Denney, *Souls of Steel* (Faith Words, New York, NY, 2008), 6-7

32. Bill George with Peter Sims, *True North* (Jossey-Bass, 2007) xxiii, Introduction

33. "Connecting the Clock and the Compass," by John C. Maxwell, February 7, 2014, johnmaxwell.com/blog/connecting-the-clock-and-the-compass

34. Kevin W. McCarthy, *The On-Purpose Person, Making Your Life Make Sense* (On-Purpose Publishing, 2009)

35. Spencer Johnson, M.D. and Larry Wilson, *The One Minutes Salesperson* (Random House Audio; Abridged edition, September 16, 2003)

36. Bill George with Peter Sims, *True North* (John Wiley & Sons, Inc., 2007), 91-92

37. Kevin W. McCarthy, *The On-Purpose Person, Making Your Life Make Sense* (On-Purpose Publishing, 2009), 84

38. MLK, Jr. and the Global Freedom Struggle, Selma to Montgomery March, 1965, *http://mlk-kpp01.stanford.edu/index.php/encyclopedia/documentsentry/doc_address_at_the_conclusion_of_selma_march*

39. Harold S. Kushner, *When Bad Things Happen to Good People* (New York: Schocken Books, 1981), 6

40. Bill George with Peter Sims, *True North* (John Wiley & Sons, Inc., 2007), 6

41. George with Peter Sims, *True North* (John Wiley & Sons, Inc., 2007), 58

42. Bill George with Peter Sims, *True North* (John Wiley & Sons, Inc., 2007), 21

43. Bill George with Peter Sims, *True North* (John Wiley & Sons, Inc., 2007), 59

44. Bill George with Peter Sims, *True North* (John Wiley & Sons, Inc., 2007), 96-97

45. "Church's Offering is "Miracle" for Charity that Serves Hundreds in Need Each Day," *Orlando Sentinel,* January 2015

46. Seth Godin, *Tribes* (Penguin Books Ltd., 2008)

47. Chuck Swindoll, *Man to Man* (Zondervan Publishing House, 1996), 260-61

48. "Great People Talk About Ideas ...," Wordpress.com, heallovebe.files. wordpress.com/2012/06/people-8.jpg

49. Scott C. Todd, PhD, *Fast Living: How the Church Will End Extreme Poverty* (Compassion International, 2011), 17-18

50. Chuck Swindoll, *Man to Man* (Zondervan Publishing House, 1996), 360-361

51. Scott C. Todd, PhD, *Fast Living: How the Church Will End Extreme Poverty* (Compassion International, 2011), 41-42

52. Ted Engstrom, *The Pursuit of Excellence* (Grand Rapids: Zondervan, 1982), 81-82

53. Chuck Swindoll, *Man to Man,* (Zondervan Publishing House, 1996), 323-324

54. "John Maxwell on Leadership," johnmaxwellonleadership.com, 2015

55. Bill George with Peter Sims, *True North* (John Wiley & Sons, Inc., 2007), 202

Made in the USA
Charleston, SC
13 February 2017